CLASSIC PALESTINIAN COOKERY

Christiane Dabdoub Nasser

Classic Palestinian Cookery

Saqi Books

British Library Cataloguing-in-Publication Data
A catalogue record for this book is available from the
British Library

ISBN 0 86356 548 4 (pb)

© Christiane Dabdoub Nasser, 2001

All colour illustrations by Bruno Marmiroli, except page 177 by Nathalie Kramoff
Original wood engravings by Fiodor Domogatsky

This edition first published 2001

Saqi Books
26 Westbourne Grove
London W2 5RH
www.saqibooks.com

Contents

Acknowledgements

My intentions for writing a book on Palestinian cuisine are both personal and practical. First, it evolved out of my interest in culinary culture in general. Second, quality Palestinian cuisine is poorly represented within Palestine and in the west. Finally, the need for a more health-oriented and less time-consuming cuisine, which draws from a heritage handed down through the generations, has become timely.

I owe my love of cooking to my mother who has managed, for the last fifty years, to keep the burner going, as it were, and it is to her that I owe my appreciation of the value of a well-cooked meal. I grew up in a home where the kitchen was the centre of activity and where a large portion of our lives was spent around the big wooden table that occupied the large central space, with my mother as queen of the realm and a source of creativity and resourcefulness. The cadence of finely cooked meals, carefully prepared and exquisitely served by her, still carries the aura of former days as we meet, children, grandchildren great grandchildren and friends, and indulge our epicurean penchants.

I also decided to write this book because of the current lacklustre situation of Palestinian cuisine and the stagnation from which Palestinian culture generally suffers, which has deprived it of its own specificity within the region of the Middle East. Palestinian identity has been crushed by the irreverent and overwhelming encroachment of a nascent Israeli 'culture' upon what is specifically Palestinian, for political ends and as part of Israel's need to secure for itself a homogenising, collective identity. This momentous period in the history of Palestine presents the right juncture for giving our cuisine its rightful place among the cuisine of other nations.

I also wanted to reflect the economic and cultural context of social groups in transition where women have joined the work force; where education has heightened awareness of health issues associated with food consumption; where travelling and cosmopolitanism among substantial Palestinian groups have prompted the need for innovation and change. The anecdotes and excerpts in the text aim to enrich the culinary experience with illustrations of cultural and celebratory traditions from different regions of Palestine.

While my mother has handed me down the principles, the inducements for keeping my family happy have given me no choice but to cook again and again, and it is to them that I owe my advancement in this field. While more than twenty years have already elapsed, I know that it is not over yet.

Finally, I owe the idea of starting this book to my friend Pauline de Laboulaye, whose suggestions and advice throughout the writing were invaluable. Also the encouragement and appreciation of my friends, who have often been guests at my table, have given me enough self-confidence to embark on such a project.

Introduction

Traditional Palestinian cuisine offers a rich variety of dishes characteristic of the eastern regions of the Mediterranean.

At a crossroads between east and west and a strategic post on the trading routes for centuries, Palestine has had its share of invasions and occupations by foreign forces. If such a tumultuous history has marked the national psyche, it has certainly served to enrich the Palestinian experience, conferring upon it the cosmopolitanism that distinguishes it from neighbouring Arab cultures, while strengthening the base that roots it deeply within the civilisations common to this geographic area. Modern-day Palestine is identified with a variety of lifestyles that cover a wide range, from nomadic migration to urban sophistication.

The establishment of many foreign communities who settled in the Holy Land in the aftermath of the Crimean war in 1855 has also contributed to the present character of Palestinian cuisine, especially in urban centres such as Jerusalem, Jaffa, Ramallah and Bethlehem. In its most recent history, especially during the last fifty years, the demographic changes that have swept the area have influenced culinary trends both directly and indirectly and although the scope of such influences are still to be determined, they cannot be dismissed or underestimated.

Palestinian cuisine, as an expression of this diversity and manifold social and cultural make-up, has shouldered the tides through integration rather than rigid resistance. Staple Palestinian dishes, based primarily on rice as a main ingredient, are a dramatic expression of this osmosis, as rice has always been an imported commodity. The cuisine of the Bethlehem area has evolved more dramatically than that of other cities, the main reason being its close proximity to Jerusalem, quite the international city since the second half of the nineteenth century, but also because Bethlehem has been exposed to outside influences in its own right. Still, due to the many villages that dot the landscape towards the south and which have close ties to the city, Bethlehem has managed to maintain rustic attributes and to happily reconcile the rural with the urban, the sophisticated with the earthy in a way that distinguishes it markedly from Jerusalem. The testimony of a nineteenth century pilgrim to the Holy Land still holds true:

> Finally, here is the city, lying in the hills and surrounded by green valleys. The white houses, vain and bright in the fading light of the setting sun, are reflections of marble against the intensity of the deep blue sky. Low walls of dry stones happily delineate the hilly slopes into terraces and gardens, cultivated in a manner henceforth unfamiliar to Jerusalem.
>
> (L'Abbé Landrieux, *In the Land of Christ*)

Lamb holds a place of honour at every festive occasion. Throughout the year, both in affluent and modest circles where every occasion necessarily gives rise to celebration, the slaughtering of a lamb is one important component capturing whole categories of cultural and social symbols that gird the fabric of daily life. Lambs are slaughtered for weddings; the occasion of the birth of a son; recovery from a long and serious illness; the return of a long absent family member or friend; the building of a new home and even the acquiring of a new car. The celebration of Easter and Adha, two major feasts based on the concept of sacrifice for Christians and Muslims alike, are a culmination of this tradition and the extended family meets around the festive table where lamb occupies the centre place. In the last three decades this practice has somewhat weakened due to several factors: urbanisation and the consequent changes in perceptions and lifestyles, economic considerations which are closely tied to a dramatic rise in the cost of living; and health awareness. However, it still persists in conservative strongholds and, more particularly, in the northern villages of Palestine where adherence to traditional practices was one of the few means of cultural expression under Israeli hegemony during the last fifty years. It also remains constant during such solemn occasions as the loss of a family member or neighbour. If the consumption of lamb has receded in favour of leaner beef or white meat, especially chicken, it still remains the basic ingredient in the rich regional cuisine and no Palestinian would ever consider honouring a guest with anything but lamb.

Samneh baladieh, or clarified butter, is another feature particular to Palestinian cuisine. During the spring season, the only time of year when the hills and grazing grounds are green and the ewes have just given birth, ewe's milk and ewe's-milk cheese are sold door-to-door. *Samneh* is strained butter that has been boiled with cracked wheat, nutmeg and turmeric, a bittersweet spice that gives the *samneh* its musk flavour and a distinctive bright yellow colour. It is one of those ingredients that cannot be bought off the shelves but has to be obtained through a network of contacts among the nomadic bedouins who breed the sheep and make the butter. The month of April witnesses the stir of housewives inquiring about prices and quality, and those who have a sure source of supply warrant their stock for the whole year before passing on the information to others. Again, due to dramatic hikes in prices and health considerations its use has been greatly reduced in favour of healthier sources of fat and many cooks use it in small amounts for flavour.

Souk, *Bethlehem*

When the milk is churned to extract the butter, the by-product, *laban mkheed*, is also processed for year-round storage. This buttermilk is left to drip through cheesecloth for a few days. The resulting pasty cheese is then kneaded with salt, cumin and turmeric, shaped into balls and dried over a wooden board in a dark room for a few days and stored in cloth bags. Individual balls of *laban jmeed*, as it is called in its new state, are diluted as needed for sauces for many traditional dishes. Bedouins in the Bethlehem area substitute the cumin with fenugreek, a highly aromatic, somewhat bitter spice.

Last but not least, it is the careful use of spices that will ultimately impart character to any cooking. The range of spices and herbs used in Palestinian cuisine has multiplied through the generations, but it is the repeated use of basic ingredients such as allspice, cinnamon, cumin and cardamom that give Palestinian cuisine its own stamp. However, whether driven by strict adherence to traditional practices or strongly tempted to experiment and innovate in search of a personalised style, Chef Escoffier's adage to 'stay simple' cannot be truer than when applied to the use of spices.

Simplicity can be certified through the quality of the spices. Careful selection – a reliable *'atar* or spice vendor is as important to secure as a good butcher – and shopping in limited quantities according to your needs for no more than two months are essential. Spices should be bought whole, as grains, sticks or roots and preserved in tightly closed containers away from any source of light or heat. Then they can be moulded, chipped or grated as needed. Luckily, buying spices in jars off a supermarket shelf is a luxury a Palestinian housewife can do without! The same goes for herbs; it is very useful to have a herb patch in the back garden or plant some select favourite ones in containers by the kitchen. Nothing equals the aroma of freshly picked herbs in a salad.

The inevitable bowl of home-pickled olives dominates every meal at every table. The olive tree is the centrepiece of every garden, however small, and is a blessed provider, needing little care and as little water. It is also an indispensable source of nutrition for every family: four trees in my garden are more than sufficient to provide for the needs of my family of six and the constant flow of family and guests for a whole year.

Formerly, preparations for the olive harvest stretched over many days of intensive work and involved the whole community, men, women and children:

> It was a busy time of year, perhaps the busiest of all, and the whole town was astir with preparations. For the men, it was an occasion for getting together, exchanging general views and speculating over the yield of this year and the profit. For the women, it involved a somewhat more strenuous effort. They would start their long day with the first light when the men and children were still asleep and before the usual morning bustle distracted them from their labour. Only late after sunset, following the return of the men from town and the communal sharing in the frugal evening meal, they could pick up their sowing or embroidery.
>
> When came the day for the harvest the whole household was up before dawn. Their eyes still swollen with sleep, the children huddled at the kitchen table sipping their tea. The women served breakfast to everyone including the *jaddadeh*, the hired hands; the hot bread from the *tabun*, lavishly smothered with the last olive oil of the year, quickly disappeared into hungry mouths.
>
> (Christiane Dabdoub Nasser, *Farha*)

The uprooting of every olive tree, practised systematically in order to advance the Israeli settler movement on Palestinian soil, is an open wound that is meant to continually deplete the symbiotic attachment of the people to the land. Today's harvests are but a caricature of former years and a brutal reminder of the history of a whole nation and its relationship to the land.

Up until fifteen years ago, it was still possible to tell the time of year from the vegetable and fruit market stalls. Nowadays, a youngster is more likely to guess the distance between Mars and Venus than the time of year to which a certain vegetable or fruit belongs. It often happens that I still wonder over a display of cucumbers right in the middle of winter when the weather is at its coldest. Mangoes in summer? Forget it. Modern agricultural techniques have erased such nostalgic moments forever.

Today, the true harbingers of the passage of the seasons are a few remaining *fallahat* who come into the towns to sell their produce out of baskets they bring in on their heads. They are tenacious peasant women who still believe in tilling their small plot according to norms inherited from their forefathers and can count on several private customers in Bethlehem, Ramallah, Hebron or Nablus. There are so few of them, however, that their name constantly circulates among the few lucky households who book them months ahead for special vegetables and fruits delivered to their doorstep. In the Bethlehem area, fresh produce comes mostly from the villages south of Bethlehem, namely Aroub, Battir, Hussan and Artas, and it carries the magic *baladi* label.

Baladi, from *balad*, country, refers to the produce of the land grown according to 'authentic' methods. In agricultural terms, it refers to products that grow on rainwater and where traditional know-how guarantees the use of natural fertilisers and a minimal use of pesticides and insecticides in order to ensure optimal flavour. It also distinguishes Palestinian produce from its Israeli counterpart, which has invaded Palestinian markets during the occupation and has led Palestinian farmers to emulate the Israeli example of mass production. The stamp of *baladi* is the local equivalent to the 'organic' label so much sought after among well to do circles in post-industrial societies.

It has been mostly due to the parsimony and conventional practices of traditional housewives that the *baladi* label has survived the last thirty years, and their menus are still largely determined by the natural cycle of the seasons. Unfortunately, however, this distinction has brought on the inevitable dictates of the basic rule of supply and demand and the constant hike in prices of *baladi* products has been frustrating to every conscientious housewife keen on maintaining the tradition. It has also led to a racket which caters for culinary snobbishness: concerned environmentalists have recently discovered that Palestinian farmers have been using four times the legal amount of pesticides and insecticides in order to secure a lucrative harvest. The concept of *baladi* has thus become relegated forever to a bygone age!

But all ills can still have their good side. A housewife feels much less frustrated at the unannounced visit of cousins from America because she does not have to depend on the casual visit of Umm Issa bringing in fresh lettuce and string beans from her plot at Artas. Nor has she to look out for the sporadic calls of Ahmad down the street promoting the excellence of his prunes and apples from Battir. No one has to rush to the garden to check if by any chance there is a bunch of *betouni* left on the trellis. There is a vendor of fruits and vegetables round every corner; failing that, the local supermarket is sure to fill in your needs with frozen products. All thanks to modernity!

This book is an introduction to traditional dishes adapted to the tastes of a wide public avid for new culinary experiences and keen on maintaining a healthy balanced diet. The recipes should be considered as guidelines and once a recipe has been tried and repeated, it is up to each cook to venture further and experiment towards a more personalised version of a favoured dish.

It is, however, worthwhile noting that when it comes to individual kitchens, what elevates plain home cooking to a gourmet feat is *nafs* and no cook can pretend to any accomplishment without it. A derivative of *nafas*, meaning soul, this essential element refers to the generosity of heart that accompanies the preparation of every meal shared with family and friends.

Finally, cooking is not just about food but also about people. There is a whole chain of men and women whose labour contributes to the final serving of a meal yet it is in the kitchen that the magic occurs. This collection of recipes is a tribute to all the Palestinian women who have embraced tradition while looking towards renewal and whose cooking is a reflection of the inherent connection between permanence and transition in a dynamic culture.

Salads

The most important principle in concocting a successful salad is fresh prime produce. This is where door-to-door selling by the women from the villages is really missed: to have a fresh tomato for breakfast right off the bush is a luxury one can only look back on. Fortunately many products are still cultivated the traditional way and some select local vegetable and fruit stores sell them on a regular basis. But going traditional also means limiting oneself to seasonal products and facing the challenge of inventiveness and resourcefulness.

Herbs are used profusely, especially mint, parsley, thyme, rosemary and coriander. Many of them grow wild and, like thyme and rosemary, can grow in rocky areas, but most homes prefer to grow their own herbs. A typical garden must feature a lemon tree, a grapevine trellis, a herb patch and the ubiquitous jasmine with its white, very fragrant flowers. The notion of cultivation for home consumption underlies every garden design and can be explained by two factors, the one practical and the other cultural. Given the perennial rationing of water and sporadic periods of severe water shortage, a garden for aesthetic enjoyment is a luxury that very few can afford. The other explanation is the vestige of an essentially *fallahin* culture that has persisted in spite of the dramatic demographic changes of the last fifty years and the rise in urbanisation and has perpetuated the notion of cultivation for private home consumption in the urban centres and their peripheries.

Garlic and onion are essentials in the preparation of most salads and their use, quite typical of the Mediterranean basin, might be considered somewhat heavy-handed by western standards. It is best to use the quantities indicated in the recipes before deciding on reducing – or increasing – the quantities, then they can be adjusted to individual tastes if it is still considered necessary.

Olive oil is ubiquitous in every salad menu. Not only is it an indispensable source of nourishment, but it also moisturises dry and pasty salads such as *hummos,* and attenuates the sharpness of others such as *m'tabbal,* which is based on grilled aubergines.

The salads presented in the following section fall under three categories according to the method of preparation: raw, cooked or dip-like. For some, preparation is simple and quick but many are elaborate and require some fine chopping that is time consuming. Do not even think of using a food processor or any other mechanical device for the chopping since the outcome is sure to be a parody of the real thing. In spite of the time and pain invested, once served these salads are the epitome of refinement, flavour and enjoyment!

Mezze refers to the assortment of sample dishes offered as a first course for formal meals, and includes a whole array of salads accompanied by relishes and hot appetisers. This tradition of assorted *hors-d'œuvres* is typical of most countries of the Mediterranean basin where *mezze* is leisurely consumed over hours of nibbling and sampling and dipping with bread. Such meals are associated with easy living, languid after-meal siestas or long summer evenings stretched-out by endless puffs on the nargileh; they also disguise the time and effort invested in the preparation of a respectable *mezze* worthy of the name!

The intensification of travel since the sixties and sustained exposure to different cultures and different foods has brought on inevitable developments that have, for the most, further enriched the local appetisers. New ingredients have been added and new dishes introduced but the base remains unquestionably Palestinian and no display deserves the title of *mezze* without the presence of *de rigueur* plates such as *hummos, m'tabbal*, beetroot salad or fried aubergines with *labneh* and pine nuts.

A good *mezze* should balance out an assortment of raw and cooked vegetable salads, grain salads and *mou'ajjanat*, pastry-based hot *hors-d'œuvres*. The variety can be substantial enough to stand as a full meal. Unfortunately, what average local restaurants usually offer is but a meagre representation of what can come out of a home kitchen where *nafs* and good 'fingertips' can whip up a variety of dishes that remain unknown to the passing visitor. To the hostess, the advantage of serving *mezze* at a seated or buffet dinner is that the various plates are all served at once, allowing her to enjoy the company of her guests without having to hover through a major part of the meal.

Most of the quantities indicated for each salad are enough for four persons, which makes it practical to include within an assortment of *mezze*.

Aubergine Salad
Salatet el-raheb

Raheb means monk. Since the origin of this salad's name remains unknown, it is believed it has been imported from Syria or Lebanon. This recipe can be accomplished by grilling the aubergines either on a stove top or in the oven. I very much prefer to put them in an old-fashioned aluminium pan the first method.

Ingredients

3 large aubergines (about 900 g/2 lb)
3 tomatoes, red and firm
salt and pepper to taste

First wash and dry the aubergines without removing the stems, then place them in a pan and grill them on high heat on top of the stove. It is possible to grill them in the oven for some 40 minutes but they do not acquire the same smoky flavour and are therefore less tasty. Turn them on all sides until the skin becomes hard and blackened, ten minutes for each side, making sure not to pierce them in the process so as to preserve the liquid. Set aside to cool.

Meanwhile, wash and dry the tomatoes and cut them up into small cubes.

Peel the aubergines carefully. The skin comes off quite easily, however make sure that none of it remains with the now soft interior. Mash the pulp and add the salt and pepper.

Serve in a deep plate and spread the chopped tomatoes over the surface.

For the dressing
3–4 garlic cloves
1 hot pepper
½ cup olive oil
3 tbs freshly squeezed lemon juice
Salt and pepper to taste
A few mint leaves to garnish

Wash the hot pepper and remove the stem and seeds. Peel the garlic. Mash them both with a dash of salt with a heavy pestle and mortar. It is possible to use a food processor, but you have to transfer the mashed garlic and pepper to a pestle to continue. Add the oil gradually, all the time working the mixture and alternating with the lemon juice. The sauce should be smooth. Add salt and pepper to taste and spoon out over the tomatoes. Garnish with whole mint leaves around the edges to form a crown.

Aubergines and Marrows with Labneh and Pine Nuts

Easy to prepare and quick to enjoy, this plate is refreshing, wholesome and has a crunchy bite to it! It can be served as an *hors d'oeuvre* on individual plates for a seated three or four course dinner or add a note of earthy simplicity to a *mezze* variety.

Baladi aubergines, the most flavoursome coming from the area south of Bethlehem, renowned for its water springs and rich soil, are tender and have a very thin skin but of short duration. *Rihawi* aubergines, so called because this variety is largely grown in the Jericho area, are available all year round and are quite tasty.

Ingredients

2 medium *rihawi* aubergines, or 500 g (1 lb 2oz) *baladi*
6–8 marrows, preferably *baladi*
½ cup oil for frying
200 g (7 oz) *labneh*
About 60 g (2 oz) pine nuts
A few lettuce leaves

If you are using the big variety, wash and wipe them dry, peel them if you prefer, although for this salad it is not necessary, then cut them into 1½ cm (½ in) slices. If you are using the *baladi,* which are small, long and thin, do not peel them, just cut them lengthwise once or twice, depending on their thickness and the way you prefer them. Sprinkle them with salt and leave them to sit for half an hour before frying them. Wash and wipe dry the marrows and cut them lengthwise into four slices each.

For the frying, you can use the oil of your choice, for years I was using corn or sunflower seed oil, saving the olive oil for salads and dressings. Lately however, because of the inherent toxins released by the different oils at high temperature, I reverted to olive oil. Fry the marrows first turning them over once after the first side is slightly brown. Place them on kitchen paper to absorb some of the frying oil. Fry the aubergines in the same way and when you are through, discard the remaining oil. Let the vegetables cool to room temperature.

Spread the fried slices in one layer on a large flat serving plate, you can use a bed of lettuce, alternating the aubergines with the marrows. Spoon some *labneh* on top of each slice, sprinkle them with the fried pine nuts and serve.

Tip
The aubergines and marrows, fried ahead of time, will have more time to drain from any excess oil if you change the kitchen paper at least once. This will give you nice and crisp but non-greasy vegetables.

Aubergines with Tahineh
M'tabbal

Large and pulpy, Jericho eggplants, *betinjan rihawi*, are ideal for frying or grilling. They are quite sharp when grilled, and intensify the flavour of many salads that accompany meat dishes. The word *m'tabbal* is the masculine passive form of spicy and its pungent flavour is due to the combination of grilled aubergines and garlic.

Together with the *hummos,* it is a basic component of the *mezze.* It can be eaten as a dip and goes very well with barbecued meat and *kibbeh.*

Ingredients

3 large *rihawi* aubergines

⅓ cup *tahineh*
⅓ cup unflavoured sour yoghurt
¼ cup lemon juice
2–3 garlic cloves
1 tbs finely chopped hot pepper (optional)
Salt and pepper to taste
Olive oil for serving, quantity according to taste
Parsley, cherry tomatoes and thin slices of lemon for garnish

First wash and dry the aubergines without removing the stems, then put them in a pan and grill them on a high heat on top of the stove. Turn them on all sides until the skin becomes hard and blackened, less than ten minutes for each side, making sure not to pierce them in the process. Set aside to cool.

It is possible to grill the aubergines in the oven for some 40 minutes but they do not acquire the smoky flavour that makes this dish such a special treat.

In a glass bowl, work the *tahineh* with the lemon juice, adding two tablespoonfuls of water if necessary to obtain a soft paste. Add the yoghurt and mix well. Crush the garlic then add it with the finely chopped hot pepper to the *tahineh*. Remember that the hot pepper is meant to add an extra edge to the salad and can be dispensed with.

Peel the aubergines carefully. The skin comes off quite easily, however make sure that none of it remains with the now soft interior. Mash the pulp and add the salt and pepper. Add the *tahineh* mixture to the aubergines and mix well. The resulting salad is soft and slightly creamy.

Spread it on a wide plate and with the back of a spoon make a circular groove for the oil. Decorate the edges with parsley leaves, lemon slices and cherry tomatoes and sprinkle with olive oil at the last minute before serving.

Aubergines with Yoghurt
Beitinjan b'laban

This salad is a variation of the *m'tabbal* with a marked difference in the flavour. The combination of the fried aubergines with the yoghurt, which gives it a smooth light texture, makes it an excellent side dish to *kibbeh b'suniyeh.*

Ingredients

3 large *rihawi* eggplants
½ cup vegetable oil
2 garlic cloves
¾ tsp salt
750 ml (1¼ pts) sour yoghurt

Wash and wipe dry the aubergines, peel them, then cut them into ½ in slices. Sprinkle them with salt and leave them to sit for half an hour before frying them. For the frying, you can use the oil of your choice, corn or sunflower seed oil or even olive oil. Fry the aubergines in a deep pan a few at a time and put them on kitchen paper to soak up some of the frying oil. You get better results if you fry them thoroughly on one side and turn them over only once. Discard the remaining oil.

I always fry them a few hours ahead, which gives me the chance to change the kitchen paper and have less greasy aubergines. It is possible to fry a large quantity and freeze some in a sealed container for later use. They keep very well for up to two weeks.

To prepare the dressing, measure out the yoghurt, add the crushed garlic and the salt then fold the mixture with the aubergine slices and stir gently, making sure not to crush them. Serve immediately. This salad wilts very quickly, that is why it is wise to season just a portion for immediate use. The fried aubergines keep very well for two to three days and the yoghurt dressing can be preserved in the refrigerator in an airtight container for 24 hours.

Avocado Salad

It is fresh, nourishing and quick to prepare! It is also as quick to disappear in hungry mouths!

Ingredients

4 medium avocados
1 whole lemon peeled
2 garlic cloves
2 tbs chopped peppers, medium hot
1 tsp salt

Peel the avocados and cut in half, removing the seed. Put the halves in a food processor and add the peeled garlic, the chopped peppers and the peeled lemon cut up in pieces and from which the seeds have been removed. Mix at high speed until you get a smooth soft paste. Served in a bowl, with crackers or *kmaj* bread on the side, this dip adds an exotic touch to the *mezze*.

Beetroot with Garlic
Salatet banjar

This salad is important to include in a *mezze* display as it adds a different dimension to the variety. The parsley, with its bitter aroma offsets the sweet flavour of the beets quite adequately.

Ingredients

7–8 fresh beetroot
2 garlic cloves
1½ tsp salt
1 tbs olive oil
¼ cup lemon juice
A small bunch of parsley, about ½ cup chopped

Put the washed beetroot in a pan full of hot water, bring to the boil and leave to cook covered for about 40 minutes. Once they are cooked rinse them out with cold water and pare them. You can dice them on a wooden board or slice them, as you prefer; the parsley has to be chopped by hand so it stays fresh all through the meal. Parsley chopped in a food processor looks limp immediately.

Crush the garlic with the salt with a pestle and mortar, gradually add the olive oil until it becomes soft and creamy. Add to the beetroot and add the lemon juice and parsley. Stir well and serve in a fresh bowl.

Broad Bean Salad
Foul m'dammas

Hummos u foul m'dammas are as inseparable as butter and jam and find their place of honour at every brunch, picnic or barbecue. It is also the poor man's staple and goes a long way when dipped with bread. The secret of a successful plate of *foul* is in its consistency, which should be soft for easy dipping.

Ingredients

500 g (1 lb 2oz) beans

⅓ cup *tahineh*
1 cup freshly squeezed lemon juice
4 garlic cloves
2 tsp salt
¾ tsp pepper
1 hot pepper finely chopped
Olive oil and some extra lemon juice for serving

Pre-soak the beans in water and half a tsp of sodium bicarbonate for a few hours or overnight. Cover them with water, cook them on medium heat till they boil, then lower the heat and let them simmer covered, for one and a half hours. Check the water and add as necessary. The only way to get the beans right is to over-cook them until they mash under the pressure of the back of a spoon against the sides of the pot. Keep on stirring and mashing for five minutes or so. You should aim for a mushy uneven texture rather than a purée. Remove from the heat and let cool for 10 to 15 minutes before you season.

Cream the *tahineh* in ¼ cup water then add the crushed garlic cloves, the lemon juice and the salt and pepper. Stir well and add to the *ful* making sure that the ingredients are well mixed. Transfer to a shallow bowl and sprinkle with the finely chopped hot pepper, some lemon juice and a generous helping of olive oil. Serve immediately as this dish is more enjoyable lukewarm.

Chickpea Dip
Hummos

Hummos is a staple food and can be eaten at any meal of the day. A substantial addition to a brunch, minced meat and pine nuts sprinkled over *hummos* can turn it into a delightful dish.

Ingredients

500 g (1 lb 2oz) chickpeas, washed and pre-soaked
¾ cup *tahineh*
⅓ cup lemon juice
2–3 garlic cloves
1 hot pepper (optional)
1½ tsp salt
Pepper to taste

To serve
2 tbs of finely chopped parsley
½ cup whole chick peas, cooked
¼ cup olive oil
Dash of cumin

Wash and soak the chickpeas for a few hours before cooking them as this will speed up the cooking process; I always cook them in the water they have been soaking in to get maximum nutritional value. Cover them with water in a deep pan and cook them until they become soft or until they are doubled in size. If you think it necessary, add some water while they are cooking. Drain, preserving some of the liquid, and set aside to cool in the pan.

Meanwhile wash and dry the hot pepper (optional) and remove the stem and seeds, as they are very irritating for the digestion. Peel the garlic.

Put half the quantity of the cooked chickpeas with some of their juice (about three tablespoonfuls) in the bowl of a food processor and add half the *tahineh*, half the lemon juice, the garlic, salt and pepper. Mix at high speed until you get a soft paste. Transfer to a bowl.

Add the rest of the chickpeas, leaving aside ½ cup for serving, the remainder of the *tahineh* and lemon juice and mix again at high speed until you get a soft paste. Add to the first batch in the bowl and stir until the *hummos* is well blended. The *hummos* should be firm but not dry, it should also be easy to spread. A tablespoonful of some of the cooking water could be used to soften the paste.

Serve on a round plate, spreading the paste while leaving a groove around the centre to contain the oil. Add the remaining chickpeas in the middle, sprinkling them with the chopped parsley, and lightly sprinkle the whole with cumin. Finally pour the oil on the surface.

Chickpeas freeze very well whole or pureed, however it is best to hold the seasoning until serving time. *Hummos* is best served at room temperature.

If meat is to be added to the dish, omit the whole chickpeas and parsley at serving and hold the oil until after you add the meat.

For the meat
400 g (14oz) minced meat
2–3 tbs of olive oil
¾ tsp salt
½ tsp pepper

Brown the meat in the oil in a frying pan on a high heat stirring constantly for even cooking; an aluminium frying pan is ideal for such purposes as it distributes the heat evenly. Once the meat is brown and crisp, it takes about 10 to 15 minutes, add the salt and pepper and immediately serve over the *hummos*. Sprinkle with olive oil.

Chickpea Salad
Balilah

Chickpeas are a favourite in cooked dishes, salads and dips. This salad derives its name from the boiled, spicy chickpeas vendors used to sell to passers-by in newspaper cones. Those were the days preceding pre-packaged chips and imported junk food.

Though high in proteins and vitamins, this salad is mostly popular because it can fill hungry mouths on a small budget. The acrid and slightly bitter taste of the cumin is an important addition to the otherwise bland chickpeas. For maximum flavour, roast a small amount of cumin seeds over the stove before grinding them.

It is possible to use canned chickpeas, but I always prefer to start from scratch. I cook chickpeas 1 kg (2 lb 4oz) at a time and freeze them for subsequent use in airtight containers. They can keep in the freezer for up to a month. Large families might need the whole amount for one meal!

Ingredients

3 cups chickpeas, cooked (see preceding recipe)
3 spring onions or 1 medium onion
1 small bunch parsley, ½ cup chopped
¼ cup lemon juice
¼ cup olive oil
1 ½ tsp salt
1 ½ tsp cumin
⅓ tsp pepper

If you are using spring onions, trim the ends while leaving a large portion of the green stems. Wash the parsley, cutting off the stems and set it aside to drain. On a wooden board, finely chop the onion and the parsley. Put them in a deep salad bowl, add the cooled chickpeas, the seasoning and the spices and mix thoroughly.

Tips
This salad is still delicious when left over, just make sure to refrigerate it in an

airtight container. Served with goat cheese or feta, on the side or diced and added to it, it makes an excellent light lunch. I have also tried using tomatoes – three tomatoes diced into small cubes for the same quantity of chickpeas – and it was equally appreciated.

Cucumber Salad
Khyar b'laban

I associate cucumbers with the long and lazy afternoons of summer holidays, punctuated by regular goings to the refrigerator when the need for a refreshing glass of cold water becomes an excuse for greedy nibbles at whole cucumbers. Unlike in the west, local cucumbers are small and tender and rather more fla-voursome, especially when home grown. No need to peel them, a dash of salt is all one needs to devour this luscious vegetable!

Cucumber salad goes very well with rice dishes. In fact, it is quite customary to serve unflavoured yoghurt with many dishes that have rice as a basic ingredient, like oriental rice and *mehshi u warak*, stuffed marrows and vine leaves.

Ingredients

6–8 cold cucumbers (750 g/1 lb 12 oz), washed and peeled
750 ml (1¼ pts) sour yoghurt
1 tsp salt
2 garlic cloves
1 tbs dried and crushed mint leaves

Cut the washed and peeled cucumbers across in thin round slices in a big serv-ing bowl. Measure out the yoghurt in a separate bowl, add to it the crushed garlic, salt and crushed mint leaves. If you are using fresh mint, a handful of chopped leaves is needed. Mix the sauce well and add to the cucumbers. Stir and serve immediately. It is also possible to serve it in individual bowls.

Tips
For an extra edge, use slightly sour yoghurt, which will offset the cool smoothness of the cucumbers. I experimented by putting this salad in a food processor and mixing it at low speed for two minutes: delicious summer soup. Omit the garlic and it can serve as pre-lunch refreshment for an informal garden party!

Fried Cauliflower with Lemon

This basic dish is a tribute to summer, when *baladi* cauliflower is abundant.

Ingredients

1 small cauliflower trimmed and cut, about 800 g (1 lb 14 oz) florets
½ cup oil for frying
½ cup chopped parsley
2 garlic cloves
2 tbs lemon fresh juice
1 tsp salt
½ tsp pepper
2 tbs olive oil (optional)

Cut the cauliflower into small florets, wash them and towel dry. Fry them a few at a time in the oil of your choice; I like to use olive oil for this particular recipe. I also prefer putting them on paper to absorb any excess oil.

Once they have cooled, add the chopped parsley, chopped garlic, lemon juice and seasoning and stir well. Cover the salad and leave for two hours. You can add two tablespoonfuls of fresh olive oil before serving.

Grilled Peppers with Coriander Dressing

Ingredients

3 sweet red peppers
3 sweet green peppers
½ cup coriander leaves
3 garlic cloves
⅓ cup olive oil
Salt and pepper to taste

Put the peppers in a pan and grill them whole – without removing the stem – in the oven for ten minutes on each side. You can use a teflon-coated pan, which you do not have to grease. When they are done, take them out of the oven and leave them to cool for half an hour before you peel them and remove the stem and seeds. Cut them in long flat strips and put them on a flat serving plate, alternating a few green strips with red ones. Wash the coriander leaves and let them drip on a paper towel; meanwhile peel the garlic cloves and chop both very finely on a wooden board. Mix the garlic, coriander and salt and pepper in the oil and add to the peppers. Serve immediately.

This salad, simple and moist, is a very good accompaniment to bread-based food such as *sfiha*.

Hot Peppers Marinated in Olive Oil
Filfil harr b'zeit

This is as delicious as it is easy to prepare. But you need to have acquired the taste for hot food. While the meat is being seasoned and the barbecue is prepared, it is a good way to get the party going, with a glass of *arak* in the other hand!

There are two ways for preparing this dish, both equally appetising.

Ingredients

300 g (11 oz) hot peppers
1–1¼ tsp salt
8–10 garlic cloves, cut in half
1½–1¾ cups olive oil

Grilled method: grill the peppers in a pan in the oven grill for eight minutes each side. Set aside to cool while you peel the garlic.

Put them upright in a jar together with the garlic cloves and sprinkle with salt. Add the oil and preserve. For best results, prepare at least 24 hours before serving.

Pickling method: Remove the stems and seeds of the peppers and cut them across in thin slices and put them in a bowl. Coarsely chop the garlic and add to the peppers, sprinkling them with salt. Transfer to a jar and cover with olive oil. Set the jar aside, away from any source of heat or light for a few days before consumption.

Tip
The leftover oil can be used to season salads or to preserve a new batch of peppers. I also use it to add some tang to grilled or steamed vegetables.

Parsley and Tahineh Salad
Bakdounsieh

Another one of the popular dip salads that accompany a *mezze* or barbecue, *bakdounsieh* is simple to prepare, flavoursome and healthy. It should be noted that it is important to chop the parsley by hand or you will end up with an unappetising dip of dubious colour and unappealing texture.

Ingredients

1 cup chopped parsley
¾ cup *tahineh*
¼ cup fresh lemon juice
2–3 tbs water
½ cup plain yoghurt
1 tsp salt
1 tsp pepper
Olive oil for serving

Wash the parsley and leave it to dry on a paper towel for a few minutes while you prepare the *tahineh*.

Measure the *tahineh* in a medium sized bowl and add the lemon juice. Work the two ingredients together until you get a fine light paste; it might be necessary to add a couple of tablespoonfuls of water to get a smooth texture. Add the yoghurt and work it some more until you get a smooth and creamy paste. Add the parsley, the salt and pepper, stir it well and serve in a deep plate. Smooth out the centre with the back of a spoon forming a trough in which you can pour enough olive oil to cover with a thin film.

Tip

Using the yoghurt with *tahineh* sauces is a trick I learnt from my mother and it helps make a smoother and lighter paste.

Potato Salad
Salatet batata

The trick in this salad is to take care not to overcook the potatoes and add the oil, lemon and seasoning when the potatoes are still warm. I like to add two table-spoonfuls of the oil left over from the hot peppers pickled in garlic and olive oil to intensify the sharpness of the onions and turn this simple salad into an event!

Ingredients

1 kg (2lb 4oz) potatoes, boiled and skinned
4 spring onions or one medium onion, chopped
½ cup chopped parsley
¼ cup lemon
½ cup olive oil
1 tsp salt
½ tsp pepper

Cut the potatoes into small cubes and place in a bowl. Add the coarsely chopped onions and chopped parsley. Add oil and lemon and seasoning. Stir and serve. If you are lucky, you will be left with some salad and it will be delicious to the last bite!

Steamed Artichokes with Garlic Dressing
Ard el-shawkeh

This treat was an excuse for a silly game that we played as young girls, picking on the artichoke leaves, like petals from a daisy.

Ingredients

4 whole artichokes, washed and steamed or boiled

For the dressing
3 tbs freshly squeezed lemon juice
⅓ cup olive oil
2 garlic cloves
Salt and pepper to taste

Once the artichokes are cooked to taste, remove them from the pan and tip them over to drain and cool, then put them on a serving plate. Prepare the sauce and serve in a separate bowl or in four individual bowls.

Tip
This salad is fun to eat among family or friends; it can be messy and therefore unsuitable for formal entertainment.

String Bean Salad
Salatet fassoulia

The best string beans I know come from the village of Artas south of Bethlehem.

For many years Umm Hilmi used to knock on our door at six in the morning bringing with her enough *fassoulia* for my mother to blanch and freeze for months to come. The same haggling over the price was repeated every year, with Umm Hilmi slightly raising her price in anticipation of this ritual and my mother, equally aware of the woman's tactics, resolved to strike a bargain.

Ingredients

1 kg (2lb 4 oz) fresh string beans, boiled or steamed
2 garlic cloves
Small bunch of parsley (½ cup chopped)
Juice of 2 lemons (¼ cup)
½ cup olive oil
1½ tsp salt
½ tsp black pepper

Mix together crushed garlic, chopped parsley, lemon juice, olive oil and salt and pepper in a small bowl. Pour over steamed and cooled string beans and serve immediately.

It is possible to substitute parsley with fresh minced coriander.

Tabbouleh

Of Lebanese origin, *tabbouleh* has been part and parcel of Palestinian cuisine for generations. One feature that marks it from its origin is the addition of finely chopped cucumbers to the ingredients. I have always done it Lebanese style and any occasion, birthday or other, provided an excuse for a *tabbouleh* afternoon party. It certainly was a star during the lettuce season for which the village of

Artas south of Bethlehem is very famous. Spoon out some *tabbouleh* onto a lettuce leaf and enjoy it with a glass of *araq* on the side.

One of the main ingredients in this salad is the parsley, which can be bought in huge bunches from the markets all over Palestine. One bunch may be enough to supply the quantity necessary to prepare a salad for six persons.

Ingredients

400 g (14 oz) parsley
80 g (3 oz) mint leaves
1 onion
4 large tomatoes
½ cup *burghol*, fine grade of cracked wheat
2¾ tsp salt
½ tsp pepper
2 tbs *sumak*
1 cup olive oil
Cup freshly squeezed lemon juice

The parsley should be washed and trimmed ready for chopping. Chop the parsley and mint leaves very finely by hand, place in a large bowl and refrigerate covered, while you prepare the rest of the ingredients.

Chop the onions very finely and put in a small bowl, to which you will add the salt, pepper, *sumak* and two tablespoonfuls of the olive oil. Mix thoroughly and set aside while you chop the tomatoes. Choose large, firm and pulpy tomatoes. Then wash and strain the *burghol*, getting rid of all the water by squeezing firmly in your hand, and add it to the tomatoes.

Add the onion mixture and the tomatoes and *burghol* to the chopped parsley and mint, add the lemon juice and olive oil and mix thoroughly. Serve in a large shallow dish with plenty of lettuce leaves on the side.

Tomatoes with Thyme
Banadoura b'za'tar

The pungent taste of *za'tar*, thyme, and the strong aroma of white cheese from sheep's milk add a particular flavour to this salad, which rouses a primeval longing for the simple life close to the earth. As long as fresh thyme is available this salad must be served at every meal. If the cheese is not fresh in season, it has to be soaked for a few hours for desalination before use.

Unlike cheeses in the west, traditional white cheese is produced in spring when pastures are available after the winter rains, and preserved in salted water for the whole year. Just like olive oil and *baladi* vegetables, the purchase of this cheese is done through a network that is continued through generations of suppliers and buyers. If a farmer holds back on the prescribed amount of gum arabic, *mahlab* and *izha*, precious ingredients that give the cheese a distinctive flavour, he loses overnight the business he has established over many years.

Although people who try it for the first time may not appreciate its pungent flavour, Palestinians who live abroad are very nostalgic for this cheese. My brother-in-law who has been living in New York for the past 40 years eats this salad heartily when his wife prepares it with feta cheese. When I asked about the English muffins he uses to dip in the sauce, he explained that it reminded him very much of *tabun* bread and that when he dips a morsel in this salad, the whole past rises from his plate. I made no further comments, but then I realised that indeed, he has been away for too many years!

Ingredients

4 large tomatoes
150 g (5 oz) semi-salted white sheep's-cheese
4 spring onions

A bunch of freshly picked *za'tar*, about 30 g (1 oz) leaves or according to individual taste
2 tbs freshly squeezed lemon juice
¼ cup olive oil
¾ tsp salt
Pepper to taste

Wash the thyme leaves and set them aside to dry on a paper towel. Meanwhile dice the tomatoes and cheese into small cubes and put them in a bowl. Trim the spring onions and chop them and add them to the same bowl.

Add the thyme leaves, the oil, the lemon and salt and pepper and stir. Serve immediately.

Tomato Salad
Salatet banadoura

Whether fried, grilled, stewed or raw, tomatoes hold a place of honour in Palestinian cuisine. It is an essential ingredient in most stews and contributes to the success of many salads. This particular salad, juicy and tangy, is a favourite and is always served with *m'jaddara*, lentils with rice.

Ingredients

4 tomatoes, washed and dried
Small bunch of spring onions (about five) trimmed, washed and dried
Small bunch of parsley, approximately half-cup when chopped
A few mint leaves
3 tbs freshly squeezed lemon juice

¼ cup olive oil
Salt and pepper to taste

Dice the tomatoes. Chop the spring onions, the parsley and the mint leaves. Put in a bowl and add the lemon juice, the olive oil and the salt and pepper. Mix thoroughly and serve immediately.

Traditional Salad
Salata na'meh

On very hot days, when appetites are stunted and minds are dulled, nothing is as replenishing as this cool, nutritious salad. It should be served immediately as it quickly wilts, especially in hot weather. It is a refreshing accompaniment to barbecued meats, grilled chicken or *kefta* and, with a *tahineh* dressing, it can stand as a light meal by itself. It moistens a *falafel* and *kmaj* sandwich. *Kmaj* is the real name for the Arabic bread known as pita in the west. Because of its shape and texture, this bread can hold a runny salad quite well, without causing any embarrassment to the person enjoying it!

Ingredients

4–6 cucumbers about 600 g (1 lb 6 oz)
3 large or 4 medium tomatoes
1 hot pepper
Small bunch of parsley (¾ cup chopped)
¼ cup chopped fresh mint leaves (or 1 tbs crushed dry mint leaves)

Classical dressing
¼ cup fresh lemon juice

⅓ cup olive oil
1 tsp salt
⅓ tsp pepper

Tahineh *dressing*
¾ cup *tahineh*
2 garlic cloves
Juice of 2 lemons (about ½ cup)
1½ tsp salt
½ tsp pepper

Wash and dry with a kitchen towel the cucumbers, tomatoes, hot pepper, parsley and fresh mint leaves. Peel the cucumbers and dice them into fine cubes and transfer them into a glass bowl; dice the tomatoes and add them to the bowl. Chop the hot pepper, the parsley and mint leaves and add them to the bowl. This part of the preparation, not in the least hard, requires some patience and, with practice, can be done in half the time.

If you are using the classical dressing, add the seasoning and spices to the salad, stir and serve immediately in a deep bowl.

The *tahineh* dressing is more substantial. Measure the *tahineh* in a small saucer, add the salt, the pepper and the crushed garlic, then add the lemon juice stirring vigorously until you get a fine white paste. Unlike other *tahineh* dressings you need not add any water, as the juice from the tomatoes will dilute the *tahineh* mixture. Mix the salad thoroughly then transfer it to a clean bowl and sprinkle with olive oil. Serve immediately.

If you are rushed for time or are entertaining guests, you can prepare the *tahineh* mixture a few hours ahead and refrigerate it in an airtight container but for best results, do not chop the vegetables and herbs more than half an hour before serving.

Soups

A friend of mine tried for a long time to get her children to eat soup and whenever she offered any all the answer she got from them was 'but I am not ill'! In Palestinian lore soup is first and foremost medicinal or a special diet for women in confinement who have to breast-feed and get the maximum nutrition.

Traditionally, a new mother spent forty days in bed and her mother-in-law, living under the same roof and dictating procedures, made sure that she was fed rich soups throughout. There was no question of her stepping out of the house before the forty days were over because her bones were still considered unsettled or 'open': '*damha m'fattaha*'; another term was '*lessaha nafas*', meaning she was still fragile. This was a far cry from the peasant woman who often delivered her child by herself, interrupting her work in the field, and walked home at the end of the day with the baby swaddled in a rag.

Armenian Yoghurt Soup
Madzuni abur

The Armenian community has been part of the Palestinian cultural mosaic for centuries. Their strength derives from their staunch spirit and their sustained pride in their language, religion and culture, symbolised by the dignified and impregnable permanence of the Armenian Quarter in the old city of Jerusalem. Although Armenian restaurants sprinkle the Jerusalem scene with exoticism, it is in the home that the elusiveness of this all too often reticent group is overcome.

Ingredients

3 cups chicken broth
½ cup rice
3 cups plain sour yoghurt
2 tbs corn flour
Salt
Pepper
1 tbs dried and crushed mint leaves

Heat the chicken broth to boiling point and add the rice; cook over low heat for 20 minutes, stirring occasionally. In a bowl, mix the corn flour in half the quantity of the yoghurt and gradually add some of the broth while stirring slowly. Add to the pot and do the same with the remaining yoghurt, ladling some soup and mixing it well before adding it to the pot. This will avoid the yoghurt from clumping in the hot soup. Cook for ten minutes than add the crushed mint. Cook another five minutes and serve very hot.

Chicken Soup
Shorbet djaj

1 whole chicken

1 medium size onion
2 garlic cloves
2 tsp salt
½ tsp white pepper
4–5 grains allspice
1 small cinnamon stick
⅓ cup rice (about 75 g/3 oz)
⅓ cup chopped finely parlsey
1 lemon cut into 6 wedges

Remove the skin from the chicken and put it to boil in a large pot in 2 litres (3 ½ pints) water, adding the peeled onion and garlic whole. Add the salt, pepper, all-spice and cinnamon and bring to the boil; lower the heat and let simmer for one hour or until the chicken is done to taste. Remove the chicken and strain the liquid in a clean pot. You can serve the chicken with yellow rice or oriental rice or an assortment of vegetables.

Add the rice to the soup and cook for 15 minutes. You may want to adjust the spices. Add the parsley and boil for another few minutes and serve immediately. The extra squeeze of lemon juice is optional and adds an extra edge to the flavour.

Cold Summer Soup

This is my own version of a summer soup, an absolute delight to quench one's thirst and provide some nourishment on hot days when appetites are low. There was one summer when I had planted tomatoes and green peppers in my garden and was proud to serve this soup right off the tree!

Ingredients

3–4 medium tomatoes (about 300 g/11 oz)
3–4 cucumbers (about 300 g/11 oz)
1 medium size radish (about 60 g/2 oz)
1 green pepper
1 hot pepper
1 garlic clove
2 cups cold tomato juice
¾ cup grated carrot
1½ tbs freshly squeezed lemon juice
1½ tsp salt
½ tsp pepper
Chopped basil for serving

Chop the cold tomatoes, cucumbers, radish, green pepper, hot pepper and garlic in a food processor and add the tomato juice, lemon juice and salt and pepper in the process. Transfer to a bowl and add the grated carrot. Sprinkle with the chopped basil and serve. You can also serve this soup in individual bowls; it makes about six servings. Serve with *qras b'za'tar,* thyme bread, and a bowl of olives.

Lentil Soup
Shorbet adass majrush

This frugal dish, once the poor man's staple, is currently appreciated on the menu of mundane dinners. Left over bread fried in olive oil was meant to stretch the meal, in the absence of any other food to complement the soup. I like to serve it with home-made croutons flavoured with garlic and olive oil.

Ingredients

500 g (1 lb 2 oz) red lentils
¼ cup olive oil
1 large onion
3 garlic cloves
2 litres (3½ pts) water
1½ tsp salt
½ tsp pepper
1½ tsp cumin

Fry the chopped onion in the hot oil until it becomes translucent, lower the heat then add the chopped garlic and continue frying while stirring until the garlic just starts to change colour. Add the washed lentils and stir, then cover with the water and leave to cook until they are tender, for about ¾ of an hour, stirring occasionally. The water level should not reach higher than halfway as it might overflow. It is also advisable to watch the pan and lower the heat as soon as it starts boiling.

When the lentils are done, mash them through an old-fashioned vegetable grinder to obtain a smooth creamy soup. Add the spices and bring back to the boil; if the soup is too thick to your liking, you can add some water and let it boil for 15 minutes. Serve immediately with croutons on the side.

For the croutons, I use whole-wheat sliced bread when *tabun* bread is not available. I rub the slices with garlic and olive oil, cut them up in small cubes and put them for a few minutes under the grill until they turn brown and crisp.

Lentil Soup with Swiss Chard
Shorbet adass b'silik

400 g (14 oz) Swiss chard
250 g (9 oz) brown lentils
1 onion, finely chopped
¼ cup olive oil
Salt and pepper to taste

Wash the lentils and cook in 1½ litres (2½ pts) of water for one hour or until they become soft.

Remove the thick stems from the Swiss chard, wash the leaves and dip them in boiling water for five minutes.

When the lentils are ready, mash them in a manual vegetable processor, leaving in the cooking pot a handful of whole cooked lentils. Add the mashed lentils. Fry the chopped onion in the olive oil and add to the pot. Return the pot to the stove and bring to the boil. Add the Swiss chard and cook for ten minutes. Remove from heat and add salt and pepper to taste. Serve immediately with wedges of lemon on the side.

Shish Barak

In Palestine *shish barak* is served as soup. In many areas it goes by the name *dinen l'ktat*, the cats' ears, and they look very much like tortellini. It is very important to have ultra-thin dough and the best way to spread it is by using a pasta machine. The traditional stuffing consists of minced meat browned with spices. I have tried adding grated celery and carrots to the meat with excellent results.

The following recipe yields about 100 bites of *shish barak* and should serve six to eight persons.

Ingredients

For the dough
250 g (9 oz) white flour
1½ tsp salt
⅔ cup water

For the stuffing
200 g (7 oz) minced lean beef
2 tbs soft butter
Salt and pepper to taste
1 celery stalk, grated (optional)
1 carrot, grated (optional)

Mix the flour with the salt and add the water gradually, each time mixing it with the flour thoroughly until all the water is absorbed. Knead and turn the dough until you get a thick smooth consistency. Set aside to rest while you prepare the stuffing.

Brown the meat in the hot oil or butter and add the salt and spices. A few minutes before removing from the heat add the grated celery and carrot and turn twice and remove. Let it cool.

If you have a pasta machine, set it to give you the thinnest dough and roll the dough through according to instructions. Otherwise spread a generous quantity of flour on your worktable and roll out half the dough until you get a very thin opaque sheet. Cut it with a 6 cm (2 in) cutter. Taking one circle of dough at a time, spoon out a scant teaspoon of the stuffing onto the dough, pull the top end over the lower end and seal the semicircle with your thumb and index finger. Join the two ends of the semi-circular stuffed dough so as to obtain a rounded tortellini. Put to dry on a floured tray or a *tabak*, a wicker tray. Repeat the same

Lentil soup

with all the dough; cover the *shish barak* and leave to dry for a few hours until cooking time. If you think the quantity is more than you need immediately, put in a zip-lock bag and freeze for up to three weeks.

For the soup
2 cups meat broth
4 cups plain sour yoghurt
2 tbs cornflour
Salt and white pepper to taste

Heat the meat broth to boiling point. In a bowl, mix the cornflour in two cups of the yoghurt and gradually add some of the broth while stirring slowly. Add to the pot and repeat with the remaining yoghurt, ladling some soup and mixing it well before adding it to the pot; this will avoid the yoghurt from clumping in the hot soup. Cook for ten minutes then add the *shish barak* a few at a time, cook for another 20 minutes, stirring gently with a wooden spoon. Season to taste and serve very hot.

Vegetable Soup
Shorbet khudra

The basic vegetables are potatoes, aubergines and marrows, available almost all year round – the marrows were preserved dried – at more or less reasonable prices. For women in confinement, boned meat was boiled into a rich broth before adding the vegetables. For families of modest means, it was a nice base for recycling leftover meat.

Ingredients

2 tbs olive oil
1 large onion, finely chopped
1 medium hot pepper, finely chopped
150 g (5 oz) chickpeas soaked overnight
300 g (11 oz) potatoes
400 g (14 oz) tomatoes or four medium ones
300 g (10 oz) marrows
1 medium size aubergine (about 300 g/11 oz)
1 large green pepper
1 tsp salt
½ tsp pepper
½ tsp allspice (or 1 tsp mixed spices instead of the pepper and allspice)
½ tsp cumin
2½ ltrs (4½ pts) water

Peel and cut the vegetables into small cubes. In a large pot fry the chopped onion and medium hot pepper in the hot oil until they just start changing colour then add the chopped vegetables and mix thoroughly. Add the spices and the water, cover and bring to the boil on a high heat. Lower the heat and let simmer for one and a half hours until the vegetables are very tender. Serve with garlic bread.

To prepare the garlic bread crush three cloves of garlic with a pinch of salt in a mortar, add while mixing constantly about ¼ cup olive oil. Brush the mixture over six slices of whole-wheat bread arranged on an oven tray and grill for a few minutes. Serve hot with the vegetable soup.

Wheat Soup
Shorbet frikeh

This soup, using very coarsely ground wheat, was a staple during the bitter cold of winter when shorter days added to the chilly darkness of poorly heated homes. A small stone grinder sat next to the earthenware silo where the wheat was stored in the driest corner of the kitchen.

On the advice of a friend I added two grains of cardamom to the recipe; her advice came as a result of many visits to Jordan where this soup is a favourite.

Ingredients

Chicken soup prepared with one chicken
½ cup stone-ground wheat
One small onion, finely chopped
1 tbs soft butter
Salt and pepper to taste
Dash of cardamom

Prepare the chicken soup using one chicken and omit adding the rice, parsley and lemon (see recipe for *shorbet djaj*). Fry the onion in the butter in a small frying pan, add the wheat and fry on low heat for 15 minutes stirring occasionally. Add to the strained soup; add the salt, pepper and cardamom and cook for another 45 minutes or until the wheat is well cooked; add some water if it becomes too thick. Serve very hot.

You can debone the chicken and serve on the side or you can save it for another meal.

Wheat

Vegetables and Vegetable Dishes

Large families with limited resources consider meat a luxury, which they can enjoy only sporadically, however they need not feel deprived as a big variety of vegetarian dishes, equally rich and equally enjoyable, can still provide them with the required daily nutrients. It is customary to cook the vegetables for a long time in order to get a soft dish that can be eaten with *kmaj* bread. Many of those dishes include a rich thick sauce, often a tomato sauce, and in spring many are based on green, leafy vegetables.

In a country that suffers from severe water shortages the cultivation of vegetables is limited to certain areas and cannot be considered as a seriously lucrative operation. After the partition of Palestine and the displacement of more than half a million Palestinians, what we Palestinians call the *Nakba*, most of Palestine's fertile areas ended up in the territory that is now Israel. The military occupation of the rest of Palestine by Israel in 1967 brought on further loss of territory through confiscation and the expansion of the settler movement. Fertile and green in the midst of bare hills of a biblical landscape, Jericho is one of the few Palestinian towns happily situated for agricultural exploitation. At almost four hundred metres below sea level, Jericho is blessed with a fertile soil, hot weather and an abundance of springs that make it ideal for the cultivation of vegetables and citrus fruits.

Jericho epitomises the demographic fluctuations that swept Palestinian cities throughout the last fifty years. A backwater of just over 3,000 inhabitants, Jericho witnessed, in 1948, an unprecedented and sudden population growth due to the influx of more than 100,000 refugees from all over Palestine. In 1967, this figure dropped dramatically as a result of the wave of emigration brought on by the Six-Day War. Today, the population of the town, including the refugee camps is 33,000.

My memories of Jericho are those of a laid back town basking in the deep folds of its lush vegetation and lulled by the steady murmur of its water springs. Little did I know of the stark conditions that marred the reality of life in the camps, all we could see as growing children and senseless adolescents was the lure of its facade. As soon as winter set in, especially during the months of January through March, it was common practice for city people to flock down to Jericho for the warm climate and green surroundings. The oldest city in the world – the Tel in the heart of Jericho is the excavation site of the urban settlement that dates back 9,000 years – Jericho shed its provincial equanimity in favour of resort sophistication for the duration of the week-end. As teen-agers we loved to throng the main thoroughfare and zoom on our bikes past colourful displays of green vegetables and citrus fruits that adorned both sides of the street, as mothers, aunts, grandmothers and godmothers paid their ritual visit to the bustling market place. Once we were back in the colder climate of the hills, out came forgotten recipes from the forlorn depths of old chests and the musty bottoms of neglected drawers. The following week promised yet another celebration of grandmothers' recipes and wondrous concoctions.

Visits to Jericho still carry some of the magic of the sixties and seventies, for all is not lost, and a culinary feast awaits enthusiasts of such simple fare as *hweirneh* and *qras b'sbanekh* – spinach cakes. The favourite fried *kiftah* meatballs that often accompany this assortment are passed over for the simpler delights of the side dishes. They brighten the dreary days of Lent when many homes, especially those of the Orthodox denomination, follow strict vegetarian and non-dairy diets. When such dishes are on the menu, the intended meagre repast turns into a gourmet special that defeats the purpose.

Whether sautéed, steamed or fried, vegetables remain favourites and endless combinations can come out of a good kitchen. After years of experience and trying out kitchen utensils, I find that a good wok is indispensable for preparing many of the vegetable dishes. Although the traditional way is to cook them till they are soft, I opt for crisper vegetables most of the time.

Artichokes with Coriander
Ard al-shawkeh ma' kuzbara

The artichoke season is limited to early summer and women get busy cutting and trimming the artichokes in order to have a nice supply of the hearts of this special vegetable in their freezers. In the last few years, it has become possible to buy them frozen in the better grocery stores at quite a high price. Preparing a small quantity is not an ordeal: wash the artichokes and peel off the leaves from the bottom with a sharp knife; cut off the upper part and core the centre clean. Always keep a basin of water laced with lemon juice to immediately soak the artichoke bottoms in so that they stay fresh and green.

Whether you buy them ready or you trim them yourself, artichoke bottoms remain a luxury dish and add a nice note to a special dinner. The heady aroma of fresh coriander leaves elevates this dish to an art form.

Ingredients

700 g (1½ lb) artichoke hearts
3 tbs vegetable oil

1½ tsp salt
½ tsp pepper
¼ cup fresh chopped coriander
3–5 garlic cloves
¼ cup freshly squeezed lemon juice

Sauté the artichoke hearts in a shallow pan in vegetable oil and cover them to simmer slowly over a small fire. Let them cook for 10 minutes adding some water if necessary. If the hearts are frozen, follow the instructions on the package before adding the herbs and spices.

While they are simmering, wash the coriander and trim the leaves from the stems and chop them finely on a wooden board. Peel and crush the garlic with a garlic press.

In a separate pan, sauté the garlic with the coriander in 2 tbs vegetable oil stirring for five minutes so as to cook them evenly. Add the garlic and coriander to the artichokes and sprinkle with the salt and pepper. Cook them for another five minutes then add the fresh lemon juice. Cook for two more minutes and remove from the heat. You can serve immediately or at room temperature. This dish can be prepared the day before and refrigerated tightly covered. Remove from refrigerator at least one hour before serving.

Aubergine with Tomatoes
Moussaka'a

Rihawi aubergines, *baladi* tomatoes and olive oil from the grove sum up in one dish the best that the land can offer. A successful *moussaka'a* is enjoyed down to the last bite for the lucky one who gets to wipe out the last trace of sauce with fresh *kmaj* or *tabun* bread.

Ingredients

2 big *rihawi* aubergines, about 800 g (1 lb 14 oz)
¾ cup olive oil
3 tbs olive oil
1 big onion
4 tomatoes
1 tbs finely chopped hot pepper
1 tsp salt
½ tsp pepper
½ tsp allspice
½ cup tomato juice

Peel the aubergines and cut across into medium-thin slices. Sprinkle them generously with salt and set them aside for half an hour. This procedure is important to reduce the amount of oil absorbed by the aubergines.

Pat them dry and fry them over a medium heat a few slices at a time in hot oil until they are golden. When they are done, remove them from the pan and put them immediately on kitchen paper. It is a good idea to take the time and effort to change the paper towels in order to allow further absorption of the oil.

Preheat the oven to 190° C/375° F/gas mark 5.

Meanwhile chop the onion into thin slices and set aside. Blanch the tomatoes by soaking them in boiling water for a few minutes to allow for easy paring. Once they are ready, remove the skin and cut them up in coarse chunks. Heat the olive oil in a pan and add the onions. Stir and fry until they are tender and translucent; add the tomatoes stirring them into the onions, then add salt, pepper and allspice. Add the tomato juice and cook for a few minutes until the sauce is ready.

Put the aubergines in an ovenproof plate and add the tomato mixture; cover with aluminium foil. Bake for 30 minutes. Remove the aluminium foil and bake for another ten minutes making sure it does not get dry. Serve at room temperature.

Chickpea Fritters
Falafel

The fast food of the Middle East, *falafel* has invaded restaurant menus of all categories in many parts of Europe and America, food kiosks in malls as well as international food festivals. It is nourishing and tasty and can be served with a variety of salads and relishes, in a sandwich, on a plate or as finger food.

Chickpeas are a basic ingredient of *falafel*. In other parts of the world, namely in Egypt, broad beans are added to the chickpeas in varying proportions. This recipe calls for uncooked chickpeas that have been soaked overnight or for at least five hours. Although frying in very hot oil is very important to prevent them from disintegrating, I have discovered that the tool used to shape the *falafel* is as essential for their success.

Ingredients

250 g (9 oz) chickpeas soaked overnight
A handful of coriander leaves, about 12 g (½ oz)
Same amount of parsley
2 hot peppers
1 small onion
4 garlic cloves
1¾ tsp salt
½ tsp pepper

2 tsp cumin
1½ tsp dry coriander

Drain the chickpeas properly and dry them with a kitchen towel. The coriander and parsley leaves have to be dried too. Remove the stem and seeds from the hot peppers; and if you care for hotter *falafel*, do not hesitate to add another pepper. Put all the ingredients in a food processor and mash at high speed for a few minutes. The mixture has to be reduced to a pulp, but it will not be smooth.

Knead the mixture and, taking small quantities at a time, shape them into small patties the size of a flat walnut. Otherwise, use a *falafel* mould if you have one; it is a small version of the hamburger mould. Drop the *falafel* patties into the very hot oil and turn them over once they turn a deep gold on the bottom side. Remove them with a perforated ladle and place onto kitchen paper. Serve hot with a traditional salad, *tahineh* sauce or garlic yoghurt, or just plain slices of tomatoes, on a plate or as a sandwich in *kmaj* bread.

Fried Tomatoes with Garlic
Kallayet banadoura

The versatile use of this dish explains its presence at tables at different times of the day. It is an interesting addition to a brunch. To supplement its nutritional value, stir two eggs with the tomatoes at the last stage of the cooking, add a dash of salt and pepper and sprinkle some olive oil. And serve a mouthwatering country-style treat that Bethlehemites call *m'thawarah*!

Ingredients

4 large tomatoes, peeled and skinned

4 garlic cloves
2 tbs olive oil
¾ tsp salt
½ tsp pepper
½ tsp allspice

Pour boiling water over the washed tomatoes and allow them to sit for a few minutes until you are able to remove the skin easily. Remove the skin and slice the tomatoes on a wooden board, making sure not to waste the juice.

Peel and chop the garlic coarsely.

Heat the oil in a shallow pan or wok and add the garlic. Quickly fry the garlic and add the slices of tomatoes, spreading them over the bottom of the pan.

Sprinkle with salt and pepper and leave to cook for five minutes. Serve immediately.

Okra with Coriander

Traditionally, Palestinians have used the seeds of coriander because of their slightly fruity taste, in recent years, however, fresh coriander, which has quite a heady aroma, is used more and more. Huge bunches of fresh coriander adorn the stalls in the market places and the shops in early summer and they can be found in the better vegetable shops all year round, which has encouraged its more frequent use in sauces and stews.

For the success of any dish based on okra, it is crucial to buy only the small tender vegetables as the bigger corns can be tough with an unpleasant texture.

Ingredients

1 kg (2 lb 4oz) okra
4 fresh tomatoes, blanched and pared
¼ cup olive oil
4–6 garlic cloves
½ cup chopped coriander leaves
Salt and pepper to taste

Trim the okra around the head as they might have a hard, fibrous crown. After washing them, place them on kitchen paper to dry thoroughly, then fry them lightly in olive oil in two batches. A wok is best for this purpose, otherwise use a wide frying-pan. While they are draining on kitchen paper, throw away the remaining oil at the bottom of the wok, wipe it with paper and add a tablespoonful of fresh olive oil, in which you will fry the crushed garlic cloves and the chopped tomatoes. Throw in the okra and cook for half an hour. Add the chopped coriander leaves, cook for another five minutes and transfer to a fresh bowl. You can serve it hot or lukewarm with *kifta,* grilled chops or broiled chicken.

Omelette with Marrows
Ijjeh

In a country that has lived through hardships and adversity, nothing is wasted and this recipe makes use of the pulp of marrows after they have been hollowed out for stuffing. It is simple and goes very well with lentil soup. I often like to include it in a brunch, especially when the *baladi* marrows are in season. This recipe can amply serve up to eight persons.

Ingredients

500 g (1 lb 2 oz) pulp of marrows
½ cup chopped parsley
1 small onion
2 garlic cloves
1¼ tsp salt
⅓ tsp pepper
½ tsp allspice
A pinch of freshly grated nutmeg
¼ tsp baking soda dissolved in 1 tbs water
8 eggs
Olive oil for frying

Wash and leave the parsley to drain. Chop the pulp of the marrows on a wooden board and transfer to a glass bowl. Finely chop the parsley, the peeled garlic and the onion and add to the marrow. It is important to do all the chopping by hand in order to avoid a mushy texture, it also avoids the loss of liquid from the vegetables.

Add the spices, the dissolved baking soda and the scrambled eggs to the bowl, stir well and let it sit covered for half an hour before frying.

Put the olive oil to heat in a deep frying pan and fry the 'ijjeh either in small individual cakes, adding to the pan a few at a time, or as a large omelette.

Tip
If you appreciate this dish, you can try using other favourite vegetables, such as cauliflower or spinach. I like to serve the larger omelettes with a topping of fresh, chopped tomatoes and garlic seasoned with salt and pepper.

Potatoes with Rosemary
Batata ma'hassa lban

Hardy and needing little care and water, rosemary grows wild in Palestine, yet its culinary value is inderestimated in our kitchens. This is most probably due to the fact that rosemary adorned funeral wreaths before the mass production of flowers and is ubiquitous to cemetaries. But I will not be dissuaded and tend to use this fragrant herb quite often and generously.

Ingredients

5–6 large potatoes
A small bunch of rosemary twigs
3–4 garlic cloves
¼ cup olive oil
1 tsp salt
White pepper to taste

Wash and peel the potatoes then cut them into thin, round slices. Arrange them in an oven pan that has been greased with olive oil. Wash the rosemary and cut off the head of the twigs where the leaves are most tender and sprinkle them over the potatoes.

In a small bowl, mix the crushed garlic cloves, the salt, pepper and the oil and spoon out the mixture over the potatoes. Place them in a preheated oven at 220° C/425° F/gas mark 7, and bake for 40 minutes. At this point you might need to add a little amount of oil if you think they are somewhat dry. Bake for another ten minutes, then put under the grill for a few minutes until they turn golden and crisp.

Puréed Marrows with Tomatoes
Mafghoussa

There is nothing more agreeable than chatting around the *tabun*, the traditional clay oven in the backyard of village homes, during the first days of spring when the easterly wind hits dry and spirits are in want of rejuvenation, catching up on the village gossip and discussing plans for the spring, while the marrows and tomatoes are slowly grilling on the last embers of the morning fire. If such a scene has been relegated to days past, the dish is still alive and cooking! A frugal dish that carries memories of the farmyard, the vegetable patch and the *tabun* is the only way to describe *mafghoussah.*

If you are an amateur of *laban jmeed*, butter-milk that has been processed and dried for year-round consumption, it will add just the flavour to make it extra special. If you prefer the cooler taste of regular sour yoghurt, you will still enjoy it to the last bite!

Ingredients

1 kg (2 lb 2oz) marrows
4 large tomatoes
1½ tsp salt
½ tsp pepper
2–3 garlic cloves
½-1 hot pepper finely chopped
1½ cups sour yoghurt

Grill the marrows and tomatoes in the oven for one hour or until the marrows are very soft to the touch. Baste the marrows with a small amount of olive oil halfway through the cooking. Let them cool for 15 minutes and cut the stems off the marrows, pare the tomatoes and mash both vegetables with a fork; you can use a food processor on slow speed for two to three minutes. Add the salt, pepper, crushed garlic cloves, the finely chopped hot pepper and yoghurt and mix well. Serve in a shallow plate and sprinkle with oil.

Serve with grilled chicken or kebab with a bowl of olives on the side.

Stir-Fried Marrows
Qouussa b'zeit

This dish, light and pleasant, can be prepared in a jiffy. I like to cook it in a wok, quite my favourite utensil for cooking many of the vegetable dishes, as well as some meat dishes such as *shawarma*.

Ingredients

1 kg (2 lb 4 oz) marrows
4 garlic cloves, mashed
¼ cup olive oil
Salt and pepper to taste

Slice the marrows lengthwise, julienne style. In a frying pan or wok, heat 2 tablespoonfuls of the oil and add half the garlic and marrows and stir fry for eight minutes. Remove to a plate and repeat with the rest of the quantities. Season with salt and pepper to taste and serve with a meat dish or as a side dish with rice dishes, such as *fattet djaj*.

String Beans with Tomatoes
Fassoulia b'zeit

This dish is delicious served fresh and warm. It refrigerates very well and can be served cold the next day.

Ingredients

1 kg (2 lb 4 oz) fresh string beans
120–150 g (4–5 oz) spring onions
2 garlic cloves
¼ cup olive oil
4 fresh tomatoes
2 tsp salt
1 tsp pepper
½ cup tomato juice (optional)
½ cup finely chopped parsley

Wash and dry the beans. Remove the string on both sides, cut off the stems and cut up the beans to desired size. Wash and trim the spring onions, cutting off the ends then chop. Peel and chop the garlic.

In a deep pan, heat the oil and add onions and stir-fry for three minutes. Stir chopped garlic into the onions and fry without browning them. Add the string beans and mix carefully, making sure that the oil wraps the vegetables in a thin film. Add the salt and spices and cook covered over low heat for about ten minutes. It is possible to add ½ cup of water if you think it necessary.

Meanwhile pour boiling water over the tomatoes for easier peeling. Peel and chop into coarse cubes and add to the pan. Cook for another 20 to 30 minutes, depending on how you like your vegetables done. If you see that the juice from the tomatoes has decreased, add ½ cup of tomato juice and adjust the salt if you think it necessary.

When the beans are tender, remove from heat and add the chopped parsley and stir. Serve warm.

Stuffed Artichokes

An Armenian dish that is best served cold it requires delicate simmering for 40 minutes on the stove top without disturbing the ingredients. It is easy to prepare and a perfect accompaniment to cold meats.

Ingredients

4 artichoke hearts
4 small potatoes
4 small onions
3 carrots
Freshly-squeezed lemon juice
Olive oil
Salt and pepper
Flour

Wash the artichokes and peel off the leaves around the base with a sharp knife. Cut off the upper part and core the centre clean. If the artichokes are big, the bottom will be wide enough to hold quite a large amount of stuffing. Soak them in water laced with lemon juice while you prepare the rest of the vegetables, as this will keep them freshly green.

Peel and wash the rest of the vegetables. Cut the potatoes and carrots in thin slices and slice the onions finely. Layer the potatoes and carrots on the artichoke heart, top with the onions and place in one layer in a large pot. Season with salt and pepper and sprinkle with the lemon and oil. Sprinkle a tablespoonful of flour and let it simmer for at least half an hour checking the liquid, and if necessary, add a small amount of water in order to allow for further cooking. When they are cooked, remove from heat and let cool. Transfer to a serving plate.

Two or three whole cloves, added to the pot, will add a rich warm flavour to the taste of this straightforward, simple dish.

Swiss Chard with Onions
Hosset silik

The best way to cook Swiss chard is to separate the stem from the leaves, which cook very quickly. You can save the stems for soup or to prepare a salad: cook the stems in salted water and when they are cooled add lemon, oil, salt and pepper and whole basil leaves. The leaves are a real delicacy and are best prepared with onions.

Ingredients

1 kg leaves from Swiss chard, washed and dried
2 garlic cloves, crushed
1 large onion
3 tbs olive oil
Salt and pepper to taste

Chop the onion finely and fry in the oil in a medium-sized pan until it becomes transluscent. Add the crushed garlic and stir for a minute or two. Then add the coarsely chopped leaves. Stir and cook over low heat for a few minutes until the leaves wilt. Add salt and pepper to taste and serve.

White Beans Casserole
Plaki

Plaki is an Armenian word that means white beans and Jerusalem Armenians refer to this salad by that name. According to Shoshane Hagopian, you cannot have an Armenian meal worthy of the name without *plaki*. Rich and tangy, it is ubiquitous at Palestinian tables.

Ingredients

300 g (11 oz) white beans, soaked overnight
6 cloves of garlic, whole
2 large carrots, sliced
1 tbs tomato paste
Salt
⅓ cup vegetable oil
¼ cup chopped parsley

In a large pot, cook the white beans until they are almost done. Make sure that they still have enough liquid and add the carrots. Lightly fry the garlic in the vegetable oil and add to the beans. Add the tomato paste and stir and let cook for another half-hour, adding the parsley for the last five minutes of cooking. Remove from heat and let cool. Serve with pot roast or grilled chicken.

Rice Dishes

Although not grown in Palestine, rice is a staple food and is unquestionably the basic ingredient in ceremonial dishes. It invariably accompanies stews and is an essential component of *mahashi*. My children love to eat vermicelli or plain rice with cold yoghurt as a snack.

Mansaf and *kidreh*, without which any celebration does not deserve any mention, are de rigueur at every traditional wedding, funeral, baptism and circumcision. *Mansaf* comes originally from Jordan but was adopted wholeheartedly by the Palestinians as a dish for special occasions, most particularly in the Hebron area. *Kidreh* is served as a rule in the Bethlehem and Jerusalem areas. They are often served the traditional way in a large, common plate, a *sidr,* and without the use of western tableware.

The Palestinian way of cooking rice is highly recommended as it allows all the water to be absorbed in the cooking process, trapping all the nutrients in the rice, unlike in the west where it is customary to strain the rice after the cooking is completed. However, it is important to be attentive during the cooking so that the rice does not stick to the bottom of the pan and therefore safer to use a griddle under the pan at the second stage of cooking.

An accomplished cook does not measure the water and is still able to get loose and fluffy rice. The trick is to add enough water to the rice to allow a wooden spoon to stand upright in the middle of the pan. I personally still prefer the measuring method, especially with the round-grain rice, which is tricky to get right, especially when the quantity exceeds a measure of two cups. For regular round-grain rice, one and a half cup of liquid for every cup of rice is the correct measure, other varieties, like Basmati or Persian or any long-grain variety, it is necessary to count two cups of liquid per cup of rice.

Most of the suggested quantities in the following recipes serve six people.

Oriental rice
Ruz hashweh

The king of rice dishes, *ruz hashweh* adorns every buffet dinner and is a favourite for all. Beautiful to look at when served, the aroma from the variety of spices makes this dish particularly enjoyable.

Traditionally, this dish is prepared with round grain rice, but I have tried using Basmati rice with excellent results. The nutty flavour of the Basmati enhances the aroma of the blend of spices that make this dish an unforgettable experience.

In the Hebron area, it is customary to add cardamom to the spices suggested in the recipe, which gives the whole dish a somewhat bitter aroma. If and when I add cardamom, I use it very sparingly and prefer to go heavy on the nutmeg.

Ideally the meat for this dish should be minced by hand. The topside is best, and you should prepare it following this procedure: cut across in thin slices like you would cut a steak, then taking one slice at a time, cut into thin strips first, then across into little cubic chips (1 cm 1/4 in).

Ingredients

800 g (1 lb 14 oz) ground lean beef

¼ cup vegetable oil
1 whole onion
3 cups round grain rice
4½ cups hot chicken broth (optional, hot water can be used instead)
1½ tsp salt
¾ tsp black pepper
¾ tsp allspice
½ tsp cinnamon
2 tsp freshly grated nutmeg
50 g (2 oz) butter

For serving
30 g (1 oz) butter
80 g (3 oz) pine nuts
80 g (3 oz) blanched and slivered almonds

Peel and wash the onion.

Heat the oil in a heavy pan, add the meat and the whole onion and fry over high heat for 10–12 minutes while stirring occasionally until the meat is nicely browned. Add the salt and the spices and cook covered over low heat while you prepare the rice.

Wash the rice in running hot water and allow it to drain, then add to the pan and stir well. Add the boiling broth or water and stir again. Cover the pan and bring to boil on medium heat. It is a good idea to taste the liquid at this point in order to check the salt and spices.

Allow the rice to simmer for ten minutes then lower the heat. You can stir the rice slowly, then leave it on low until most of the liquid is absorbed. If you prefer put a griddle under the pan to prevent the rice from sticking to the bottom.

When the rice is almost done dot the surface with the butter and cook for another five minutes. Remove from heat and cross the bottom of the pan with a wooden spatula in order to distribute the butter without squashing the rice. Allow it to rest covered for a few minutes before serving. Meanwhile, brown the almonds and the pine nuts separately, in the butter in a pan over medium heat, stirring so as to get an even golden colour. Spread evenly over the rice.

Served with broiled or charcoal-grilled chicken, this meal becomes a real treat.

Tips
To avoid lumpy rice, put a clean kitchen towel under the lid covering the pan while it rests.

To add some flair to your dish, wrap individual portions of the rice and nuts in puff pastry (unsweetened) and put those portions on a greased pan and bake on medium-high heat for 30 minutes or until they become golden brown. We call them *bukaj*, meaning the knotted kerchief in which travelers used to put their belongings.

Plain Rice
Ruz m'falfal

Easy to prepare, this rice is usually served with stews. It is traditional to use the round-grain rice, readily available and much cheaper. I like to use Persian or Basmati rice occasionally for variety. You can cook this rice with chicken or beef for a richer flavour.

Ingredients

2 cups rice
30 g (1 oz) butter

3 cups broth
¾ tsp salt
Dash of white pepper

Wash the rice under the hot water tap and drain it. Dissolve the butter in a small pan, add the rice and mix thoroughly with the butter. Add the salt and pepper and the broth, stir and bring to the boil, leave covered for a few minutes. Reduce the heat and cook for another 10 - 15 minutes, until the rice is cooked and all the liquid is absorbed. Remove from heat and let it rest for five minutes before serving.

Rice with Beef and Cauliflower
Makloubet zaher

Makloubeh means upside down with reference to the way it is served; it is as wholesome as it is filling and is regularly served in large families. The vegetables included in this dish are usually fried aubergines or cauliflower or both. The rice is layered with the meat and vegetables and when the cooking is done, the pan is tipped over a plate or tray to serve. I use an old-fashioned aluminium pan with slanted sides, wider at the top and without handles, which makes for easier tipping.

I prefer to use either cauliflower or aubergines and have tried it with marrows with great success. One basic rule is to go totally traditional: use mutton and fry the vegetables – I have tried to sauté the vegetables lightly but the casserole came out dry and the ingredients did not blend smoothly.

In spring and early summer, when the *baladi* aubergines from Battir are out, this dish is cooked quite often until *el-ghbar*, when the baladi aubergine season is over. Battir aubergines, unlike the brands that originate from Jericho or Gaza, are small and narrow and quite light in colour, they also have a thin skin making their peeling unnecessary.

This dish is best accompanied by yoghurt or yoghurt based salad.

Ingredients

1 kg (2 lb 4 oz) of beef, trimmed and cut in chunks
1 whole onion, peeled
3–4 tbs olive oil or 30 g (1 oz) *samneh*
2 tsp salt
1 tsp pepper
¾ tsp allspice
1 small cinnamon stick
(You can substitute the pepper, allspice and cinnamon with 1½ tsp mixed
    spices)
1 small cauliflower cut into florets or 8 small aubergines, washed and dried
½ cup olive oil
2 cups round grain rice
1 tbs *samneh* or clarified butter
At least 3 cups of hot water (less if you add the meat juice)
Salt and pepper to taste

In a large pan, brown the meat with the onion in the hot oil or *samneh*. Add the salt and spices and enough water to cover the meat. Bring to boil then let it simmer covered for 60–70 minutes. The amount of time can vary according to the type and cut of meat you use and to the degree you like it done.

While the meat is cooking, fry the cauliflower in a separate pan in ½ cup olive oil until the florets are soft and golden. Let them drain over kitchen paper.

If you are using aubergines, peel them and cut them into slices of desired thickness. If you are using small oblong aubergines just cut them lengthwise in two. Heat the oil in a separate pan and fry them, turning them only once. Place the fried slices on kitchen paper until the meat is ready.

Measure the rice and wash it under the hot water tap. Leave it to drain. Melt the butter or *samneh* in a large aluminium pan, add the rice and stir until all the rice is coated with the butter. Remove half the rice and even out the rice at the bottom, add a layer of the fried cauliflower or aubergines, and add the chunks of meat saving the juice. Add the remaining rice and top with a layer of the remaining vegetables. Measure the liquid of the meat and add enough hot water to make three cups. Bring to boil on a high heat with the pan covered. Taste a spoonful of the liquid to adjust the spices. Lower the heat to medium and cook for 15 minutes. Add an insulating griddle under the pan and leave to cook until all the liquid is absorbed. Turn off the heat and let it rest for five minutes before serving.

Rice with Mutton and Chickpeas
Kidret hummous

This *kidreh* dish is a variation on the Bethlehem version and is very popular in the Ramallah and Bir-Zeit areas as well as in coastal Gaza where cumin, much more freely used, enhances the blandness of chickpeas with a warm and slightly bitter flavour. For best results, it is advisable to grill the cumin seeds in a small pan and grind them just before use. Otherwise, it is a good idea to grill and grind small quantities at a time and save them in a tightly covered jar away from any direct source of light or heat. This principle applies to all spices if you want to obtain optimum results.

The cooking process is similar to western style casseroles where all the ingredients are cooked in the same pan. The best way to serve this dish is with plain yoghurt on the side. It is quite a treat!

Ingredients

1 kg–1.2 kg (2 lb 4 oz–2 lb 11 oz) mutton, cut up in chunks
1 whole onion
2 tbs clarified butter
2½ tsp salt
1 tsp pepper
½ tsp allspice
1 small cinnamon stick
400 g (14 oz) cooked chickpeas
2 cups rice, round grain
3 cups hot water
4 garlic cloves
1½ tsp cumin
50 g (2 oz) butter

In a large pan, brown the meat with the onion in the butter.

Add the salt and spices and enough water to cover the meat. Bring to boil then let it simmer for 60–70 minutes. The amount of time can vary according to the type and cut of meat you use. It is to be noted that lamb cooks faster than beef, however it is always better to consult with your butcher. When the meat is done, add the cooked chickpeas and heat through.

Measure the rice and wash abundantly with hot water. Add to the pan and mix with the meat and chickpeas. Measure the hot water and add to the pan. If there is already some liquid from the meat, you might not have to use all three cups of water otherwise you will end up with sticky rice.

Melt the 50 g of butter in a pan and add the peeled and crushed garlic with the cumin. Fry for three to four minutes and add to the rice mixture. Mix carefully with a wooden spoon, lower the heat to medium and leave to cook covered for ten minutes. Add an insulating griddle under the pan and cook slowly until all the liquid has been absorbed, about five minutes or so.

Turn off the heat. Uncover the pan and place a fresh kitchen towel over the top and replace the lid. Leave to rest for five minutes before serving. The cotton towel will absorb the extra moisture and prevent the rice from getting sticky.

Rice with Chicken and Yoghurt
Fattet djaj

Nutritious and filling, this dish is served with *tabun* bread soaked in chicken broth, whence the name *fatte*. I prefer to use *tannur* bread, round, flat bread lighter and thinner than *tabun*, and spongy enough to absorb the broth. Palestinians have traditionally served their favourite dishes with different breads, not unusual in a country that has witnessed long stretches of hunger.

Although *fatte* is still a special meal for most families, it is served in some circles to reflect the new trend for going traditional. The following recipe serves a party of eight to ten people.

Ingredients

2 chickens
1 onion
1½ tsp salt
1 small cinnamon stick
2 bay leaves
¾ tsp pepper corns
6–8 grains allspice
Dash cardamom grains (optional)

20 g butter (1 oz) for the chicken
3 cups round grain rice
40 g butter (1½ oz) for the rice
2 oz blanched and slivered almonds
2 oz pine nuts

Cut the chicken in four and remove the skin. Put in a big pan and add the salt and spices and enough water to cover. Bring to the boil and let simmer for one hour or until the chicken is tender. Strain the broth and set it aside for the rice.

Melt the butter in a saucepan and add the rice after it has been washed under a hot water tap. Measure out 4½ cups of the hot chicken broth leaving two cups for serving the bread, add to the rice, cover the pan and bring to the boil. It is important to taste the liquid and adjust the seasoning before all the liquid is absorbed. Keep on medium heat until most of the water is absorbed, about 15 minutes. Reduce the heat and let it simmer for another three minutes. Remove from heat and set to rest for a few minutes before serving.

While the rice is cooking remove the bones from the chicken and spread the boneless meat on a greased tray, dotting it with small pieces of butter; put in the broiler for ten minutes while you fry the almonds and pine nuts in a small amount of butter.

In a large serving plate, or a *sidir*, spread three of the warmed *tannur* bread, which is usually about 30 cm (12 in) in diametre and ladle out the hot broth over the surface. Top with the rice and spread the chicken over the surface. Add the almonds and pine nuts and serve with *laban m'thawam.*

To prepare the *laban,* add three garlic cloves crushed with ¾ tsp salt with a pestle and mortar to three cups of sour yoghurt.

Rice with Lentils
M'jaddara

The proverbial poor man's dish, it took me quite a few years before I started appreciating it; now I can eat *m'jaddara* with a simple tomato salad on the side any day.

There are two types of lentil grains, flat ones and round ones, *adas baladi*. The latter are tastier and cook faster. I always opt for the *baladi* though they need more attention to come out just right.

Just like the other rice dishes, the cooking water of the lentils should be totally absorbed, trapping all the nutrients in the prepared dish.

Ingredients

1 cup lentils
½ cup rice
1½ tsp salt
¾ tsp pepper
1½ tsp cumin
1 onion
¼ cup olive oil

Wash the lentils under the running tap. Put them in a cooking pan with just one cup of water and bring them to boil on a high heat, it takes about five to seven minutes. Lower the heat and cook them covered for another 15 to 20 minutes or until all the water is absorbed. Add the washed rice, the salt, pepper and cumin, add another cup of water, stir gently and leave to boil, then lower the heat. At this stage of the cooking you can put a grid under the pot in order to make sure that the rice and lentils will not stick to the bottom of the pan.

Rice with mutton, kidreh

While the lentils are cooking, peel and wash the onion and chop it into rings. Heat the olive oil in a frying pan and fry the onion rings until they turn golden. By this time, the cooking water of the lentil and rice mixture will have been almost absorbed: add the hot oil from the pan to the lentils, but do not add the onion rings, and stir gently with a wooden spatula. Leave it to simmer for a few more minutes until the liquid is totally absorbed, then remove from the stove and leave to rest for a few minutes before serving.

Use the onion rings to decorate the top of the serving plate and prepare a tomato salad to serve on the side.

Rice with Mutton
Kidreh

When the wedding feast was cooked, the men gathered around to eat from the large trays of meat and rice. The following song was sung to them:

Our bread is sufficient, our house is warm
Our sword is perfect!
Eat ye good men of God!
May it do you good.

After the men had eaten, the food was carried to the women, who had been sitting with the bride.

(Seger, *Granquist*)

Originally, *kidreh* referred to a split level clay heater used formerly for cooking, then it came to mean a brass or clay container shaped wide at the bottom with a narrow opening, which was traditionally used to cook this dish, whence the name. During ceremonial occasions when the extended family as well as friends are present, it has become customary to have it catered. They would come with as many *kidrehs* as were ordered, steaming straight from the wood oven and the fragrance of spices and *samneh,* lavishly used for the occasion, would fill the air.

For funerals or other sad occasions, a one-course meal of *kidreh* and yoghurt is served to all the members of the family, the clan and all the friends and acquaintances. It is a social obligation the family of the bereaved has to honour, even if it means borrowing money.

For large parties, this dish is preceded with all sorts of appetisers and salads, and followed by a *sidir* of *knafeh*, a traditional cheese dessert from the Nablus area. Back in the thirties, when my aunt got married to a Palestinian who had emigrated to Chile and had come back to Bethlehem to find a bride, my grandfather, who was well travelled and had lived in France for many years, held two banquets for the occasion. The first was traditional in order to save face with the family and clan members who expected nothing more nor less than the traditional *kdur* (plural of Kidreh). For his friends and acquaintances in Jerusalem, already more worldly and among whom were many foreigners, he served a Western style banquet with china and silverware and for dessert, delicate French pastries ordered from a Jewish bakery in Jerusalem. At that time, Western-style wedding dresses had already made a breakthrough since the mother of the bride, my grandmother, had a white weddingdress instead of the traditional *thowb malak*.

Ingredients

1 kg–1.2 kg (2 lb 4 oz–2lb 11 oz) mutton cut up in chunks
2 bay leaves

2½ tsp salt
1½ tsp pepper
1 tsp allspice
¼ tsp nutmeg
⅛ tsp cardamom
2 cinnamon sticks
(You can substitute the above spices with 2½ tsp mixed spices)
1 onion
3 cups round grain rice
4½ cups broth
¼ tsp saffron pistils
4 garlic cloves
50 g (2 oz) butter or 2 tbs *samneh*

It is best to use chump chops or a shoulder cut, but you can also use the leg. Traditionally, the meat is cooked with minimal trimming of the fat but I prefer to have it trimmed as much as possible and to skim the fat off the juice before adding the rice.

Put the chunks of meat in a medium-size pan adding the whole peeled onion and the salt and spices. Cover with water and cook for 1¼ – 1½ hours, or until the meat is tender.

For the second stage of the cooking, use a big cast iron or heat-resistant clay pot. Grease the bottom and sides of the pot with butter or *samneh*. Wash the rice under the hot water tap and leave it to soak for five minutes before transferring it to the pot. Meanwhile crush the garlic with ¼ tsp salt to a fine paste in a pestle and mortar then soak the saffron for a few seconds in a small amount of hot water. Measure the meat broth and the saffron liquid and add enough hot water to make 4½ cups and pour over the rice in the pot. Add the crushed garlic and the butter or *samneh* and stir. Add the chunks of cooked meat on top, cover the pot and put in a moderately hot oven (200° C/400° F gas mark 6) for half an hour, when you check if the rice is done and all the liquid has been absorbed. If necessary, leave it for another five minutes or so. Serve with plain sour yoghurt and simple traditional salad on the side.

Rice with Mutton and Yoghurt
Mansaf

Originally from Jordan, this dish is cooked in a variety of ways according to the different regions, but it is in Hebron that it has become established as the dish to surpass all dishes, and is always served to dignitaries and official guests. A stronghold of tradition and conservatism, Hebron society entertains the traditional way, with the men separated from the women. The *mansaf* is served in a large *sidir*, a big round brass platter without western tablewear. The men will stand alone in a circle around the *sidir* and eat while the women of the house are in the kitchen. On such occasions, it is the duty of the man of the house to make sure that his guests are not in want of anything.

Ali Qleibo, an anthropologist friend of mine, describes the ritual of sharing *mansaf* most accurately:

Each food morsel is transformed, with an elegant well coordinated movement of the thumb, index and middle fingers, into an oval shaped mouthful. In the elegant hands of an expert, not a single grain of rice slips in the process of tossing the morsel into the mouth.

(Ali Kleibo, *Before the Mountains Disappear*)

Mutton, *laban jmeed*, dry yoghurt from lamb's milk, and cardamom are specific ingredients for this dish. The distinctively pungent taste of the *laban* and the bitterness of the cardamom may not appeal to every taste. I have developed my own version of this royal dish substituting the *laban jmeed* with plain yoghurt and using a hint of cardamom.

Ingredients

1 kg–1.2 kg (2 lb 4 oz–2lb 11oz) lamb, cut up in large chunks for stew
1 whole onion
2 tsp salt
1 tsp pepper
¾ tsp allspice (you can substitute the pepper and allspice with 2 tsp of mixed
    spices)
3 tbs clarified butter
2½ cups round grain rice
2 tbs *samneh* or butter
⅛ tsp saffron flowers or powdered turmeric
3 grains cardamom

For the sauce
200 g (7 oz) dry yoghurt (*laban jmeed*) or three cups sour yoghurt + 2 tbs
    cornflour
2 cups broth
3 whole garlic cloves
1 tsp butter or *samneh*

For serving
1 large *tannur* bread
20 g each fried pine nuts and almonds for topping

If you are using *laban jmeed*, soak it for 24 hours with enough water to cover the clumps of *laban*. When the *laban* has absorbed all the liquid and the clumps have softened, process in a food processor for a few minutes until you obtain a thick liquid of creamy consistency. In the old days, they used to soak the *laban* for a few hours in water and rub the clumps by hand against the rough bottom of an earthenware bowl, hence the other name by which it is also known, *laban san*. It took a great deal of elbow grease to prepare enough *laban* for a large family! You can prepare the *laban* a day ahead, you should obtain about three cups, and keep in the refrigerator.

Sprinkle the chunks of meat with the salt, pepper and allspice. Put the meat in a medium-size pan, add a small cinnamon stick and the peeled onion and cover with two litres of water. Bring to the boil and cook covered until the meat is tender, about one hour. You might have to skim the foam off the surface. When the meat is ready, keep it hot in the pan while you cook the rice. You will need two cups of the broth for the sauce and the rest will serve to cook the rice.

Heat the *samneh* or butter in a medium size cooking pot and add the rice and the grains of cardamom. Stir until all the rice is coated with the fat. Add the saffron diluted in two spoons of hot water or the turmeric powder and stir once again. Measure four cups of liquid using as much broth as there is available, topping with hot water, and add to the rice. Bring to the boil and adjust the seasoning. Cover and cook over medium heat until most of the liquid is absorbed. Reduce the heat and cook for another five minutes before turning off the heat. You can use a griddle during the last stage of the cooking in order to prevent the rice from sticking.

You can prepare the *laban* sauce while the rice is cooking: melt the butter in a medium size pan and add the garlic. Stir over low heat while making sure that the garlic does not change colour. Add the *laban* and broth and cook for 20 minutes over a very low heat. Add salt and pepper to taste. If you are using yoghurt, mix in the cornflour in the yoghurt and add the hot broth a small quantity at a time to avoid any lumps. Heat through on a low flame and adjust the spices if necessary. Turn off the heat and everything should be ready for serving.

Spread the hot bread on a large round tray and spoon over it at least one cup of the hot *laban* sauce. Serve the rice making sure to remove the cardamom seeds and spoon out some more sauce serving the rest of the sauce in a small bowl for extra servings. Arrange the meat over the rice and add the almonds and pine nuts. You can prepare individual bowls of hot *laban* as a side plate.

Bon appétit!

Saffron Rice
Ruz 'usfour

Saffron, the most precious of all spices, gives this simple dish a powerful aroma and smooth warm taste. I like the nutty flavour of Basmati rice for variety.

It takes 150,000 flowers to yield 1 kg (2 lb 4 oz) of saffron, which raises the price of this exotic spice remarkably. Turmeric may be used as a substitute as it has the same slightly bitter and musky aroma. In case you want to invest in saffron, buy the flowers as opposed to the powder, which is often adulterated to make it more lucrative.

Ingredients

1 small onion finely chopped
50 g (2 oz) butter
2½ cups Basmati rice
2 tsp salt
¼ tsp saffron
4 cups boiling water

Melt the butter in a pan over a medium heat, add the chopped onion and stir until it becomes translucent. Add the rice and salt and measure the water. Soak the saffron pistils in a small amount of water for five minutes.

Bring to the boil, covered, and keep on a medium heat until most of the water is absorbed, about 12 minutes. Reduce the heat and add a grid diffuser let it simmer for another three minutes. Remove from heat and allow to rest for a few minutes before serving.

Vermicelli Rice
Ruz b'sh'ayrieh

¾ cup fine noodles, crushed
4 tbs vegetable oil
2½ cups round grain or long grain rice
3¾ cups boiling water/5 cups for the long grain
1 tsp salt
¼ tsp white pepper
1 tbs butter

Measure the rice and wash it under the hot water tap. Leave it to drain.

In a pan, stir-fry the noodles in the oil until they turn golden. Add the rice and stir quickly, then add the salt and pepper.

Measure the hot water according to the type of rice you are using, add to the rice and bring it quickly to boil. Lower the stove to medium heat and let it cook until most of the water is absorbed, about 12–15 minutes.

Dot the rice with the butter and leave to cook for another three minutes. When it has melted, remove from heat and, instead of stirring, cross the bottom of the pan with a wooden spatula to spread the melted butter without squashing the rice. Leave it to rest for a few minutes before serving.

A side dish for most stews, this rice is also delicious with plain yoghurt. My children snack on vermicelli rice with yoghurt at all hours.

Stews

Stews are basic fare for everyday family cooking and are always served with vermicelli rice or plain rice. They are popular because they provide a wide range of nutrients from the meat, the vegetables and the rice, and supply the extra liquid so essential in a climate where dry weather is the norm for most of the year. The other explanation is purely economic as a relatively small amount of meat can go a long way into feeding a large family, especially during hard times and among the poorer population.

Stews are traditionally cooked with lamb or mutton, mostly untrimmed of the fat, although recently beef has come to replace lamb among the health conscious. Lamb is more tender and presents a wider choice of cuts; whether from the middle neck and shoulder, the shank, the loin or around the rib, the cuts are most likely to be juicy and appetising. The choices are more limited with beef, and depend on the grade of beef a cook can afford. The chuck or rib is generally standard for stews and requires longer cooking time than the lamb; also the meat comes out chewy.

In a traditional kitchen the meat is first boiled with the spices and later fried in *samneh*, clarified butter to which special spices have been added. This procedure is ideal for lamb. However with beef, it is advisable to brown the chunks on a high heat first in order to seal the juices and obtain softer, less chewy meat. As the use of *samneh* has also decreased for health reasons – it is totally absent from many kitchens – a teaspoonful can be added at a later stage in the cooking for the flavour.

In the preparation of stews, it is mostly the spices that give the dish you are preparing its particular Palestinian stamp. While pepper and allspice are the standard, nutmeg, cinnamon, cloves, cumin and coriander – I also like to add a hint of cardamom – are essential, but in very small quantities. It is therefore a good idea to keep a small jar of a mixture at hand, just enough to suit your need and the use you are going to make of them. For the recipes that need an additional quantity of a specific spice, it will be indicated in the ingredients.

Cauliflower Stew

This recipe is easy and can be prepared quickly. While it is not usual to prepare stews with minced meat, it was one way to convince my children to eat it when they were little. I cut the cauliflower in small florets; and eating this dish soon became an amusing adventure into a secret garden. Aida Shehadeh, who originally gave me the recipe, cooks it for them while they are visiting her in Paris. Of course, she keeps her own supply of spices, which she replenishes from her usual *attar,* the spice vendor, at every visit to Palestine.

Ingredients

One head of cauliflower
¼ cup vegetable oil
500 g (1 lb 2 oz) lean minced beef
1 medium onion
3 tbs vegetable oil

1 tsp salt
¾ tsp pepper
⅓ tsp allspice
⅛ tsp cumin
1 cup broth
(You can substitute the pepper and allspice with 1 tsp mixed spices)

Wash and dry the cauliflower. Cut into small florets, saving the rest of the vegetable for soup. Heat the ¼ cup oil in a wok and stir-fry the cauliflower in two batches or more, depending on the size of your wok. As you fry and stir, be careful not to break the florets. Leave the cauliflower to drain on kitchen paper while you prepare the meat.

Peel the onion. In a medium size pan heat the three tablespoonfuls of oil, add the onion and the minced meat and brown while stirring. Add the salt and spices and cook for another few minutes. Add the cauliflower and broth and cook covered for 15 minutes. Serve very hot with vermicelli rice and a simple tomato and cucumber salad on the side.

Jew's Mallow
M'loukhiyeh

M'loukhiyeh, or Jew's mallow as it is known in certain countries in the west, is a green vegetable that grows into long thin stalks with dark green leaves that have a somewhat acrid taste. The marriage of fresh coriander, with its sweet aroma, with the *m'loukhiyeh* makes this dish quite unique. You can also add coriander seeds, different in taste from the fresh leaves in that they are slightly peppery.

In Palestine, dry coriander is more commonly used than the fresh leaves. Until recently, I have always favoured using the fresh leaves, perhaps influenced by my partly Syrian roots. However, at the advice of a friend, I have recently grown accustomed to add a dash of the crushed dry seeds to balance the aroma of the leaves.

Ingredients

1 kg (2 lb 4 oz) of beef or lamb, cut in chunks for stew
¼ cup vegetable oil or 30 g (1 oz) butter
1 whole onion
2 tsp salt
1 tsp pepper
¾ tsp allspice
1 small cinnamon stick
(You can substitute the pepper, allspice and cinnamon with 2 tsp mixed spices)
400 g (14 oz) leaves of *m'loukhiyeh,* Jew's mallow, washed and drained
⅓ cup freshly squeezed lemon juice
6–8 garlic cloves
1 medium sized bunch of fresh coriander +1 tsp of dry coriander seeds, crushed
1 tbs butter

In a large pot, brown the meat with the onion in hot oil on a high heat. Add the salt and spices and enough water to cover the meat. Cover the pot and bring to boil then let it simmer on a low heat for 60–70 minutes or until the meat is cooked to your liking. The amount of time can vary according to the type and cut of meat you use, and to the way you like it done. Palestinians favour meat that is very well cooked and tender.

While the meat is cooking, finely chop the *m'loukhiyeh,* by holding the leaves length- wise in small bunches and cutting across with a sharp knife. Squeeze the lemons and chop the coriander leaves and the peeled garlic in the food processor.

As soon as the meat is done, remove the pieces and transfer to a serving plate and keep covered in a warm place until the *m'loukhiyeh* is ready. Add some water to the pot if you think it is not enough to cook the *m'loukhiyeh* leaves: you need at least one and a half litres of liquid. Add the lemon juice to the meat sauce, bring to the boil and add the chopped *m'loukhiyeh*. Leave to cook for ten minutes uncovered.

Meanwhile melt the butter in a small frying pan and fry the garlic, the coriander leaves and the dry coriander for three minutes while stirring. Add to the stew and cook together for another five minutes. Serve immediately accompanied by the meat, plain rice, *ruz m'falfal*, bread croutons and vinegar dressing.

The croutons are home-made from plain, grilled bread cubes. For the dressing, finely chop a medium-sized onion to which you add a dash of salt, the juice of one lemon and half a cup of white vinegar.

It is best to serve this stew in soup plates. Start with some bread croutons in the bottom of the plate and ladle out some of the stew, then serve the rice over the *m'loukhiyeh*, top with some more stew and meat and sprinkle some vinegar dressing. *Saha u 'afieh*! Enjoy!

Tips

It is important to add the lemon juice before the leaves in order to prevent the *m'loukhiyeh* from becoming runny.

After adding the *m'loukhiyeh* leaves, cook uncovered in order for the juice and the leaves to blend well.

Okra Stew
Yakhnet bamieh

This is a long-time favourite. The tomato and garlic sauce brings out the tangy taste of the okra.

Buying okra in the local markets is an exercise in patience as it is important to select the small tender ones as they are less chewy, which means you have to get up early and hit the vegetable stalls while the farmers are still unloading their boxes of fresh produce. If you are lucky, you may have your own neighbourhood supplier who can bring it fresh from the fields to your door. Even if they are not small enough to your liking, their freshness is enough of an incentive to make you buy the whole lot. You cook what you need and freeze the rest, either through blanching or frying, to use when they are out of season.

Ingredients

1 kg (2 lb 4 oz) beef or 1–1.2 kg (2 lb 4 oz–2 lb 11 oz) lamb cut up in chunks
 for stew
1 whole onion
3–4 tbs vegetable oil
2 tsp salt
1 tsp pepper
¾ tsp allspice
800 g (2 lbs) fresh okra
3 tomatoes
1 green pepper
1 hot pepper (optional)
4 garlic cloves
3 tbs olive oil

2 tsp salt
½ tsp pepper
⅓ tsp allspice

In a large pan, brown the meat with the onion in hot oil. Add the salt and spices and enough water to cover the meat. Bring to boil then let it simmer for 60–70 minutes. The amount of time can vary according to the type and cut of meat you use. It is a good idea to consult with your butcher.

Meanwhile wash and dry the okra. The traditional practice is to fry it before adding it to the meat so as to avoid it getting sticky. As okra absorbs too much of the oil, it is important to let it sit on kitchen paper for a while before adding it to the meat. I prefer to add it raw and leave it to cook uncovered on medium heat for half an hour or until the okra is almost tender.

While the okra is cooking, peel and chop the tomatoes, and chop the green pepper and hot pepper after having removed the stems and seeds. The seeds of the hot pepper can be quite irritating for the digestion and it is important that they be entirely removed. Peel the garlic and chop it finely, or crush it in a garlic press.

In a large frying pan, heat the olive oil and add tomatoes, peppers and garlic. Add salt and seasoning and fry uncovered for five minutes.

Add to okra and cook for another five minutes.

This stew is best served with vermicelli rice.

Unlike in the West, Palestinians prefer their vegetables well cooked. Individual taste should determine the length of cooking for the vegetables; however, I find that okra is tastier with longer cooking.

Pea Stew
Yakhnet bazela

1 kg (2 lb 4 oz) beef or 1 kg–1.2 kg (2 lb 4 oz–2 lb 11 oz) lamb, cut up in chunks
    for stew
1 whole onion
3–4 tbs vegetable oil
2 tsp salt
1 tsp pepper
¾ tsp allspice
1 small cinnamon stick
800 g (2 lbs) fresh or frozen peas

In a large pan, brown the meat with the onion in hot oil. Add the salt and spices and enough water to cover the meat. Bring to boil then let it simmer for 60–70 minutes. The amount of time can vary according to the type and cut of meat you use. It is a good idea to consult with your butcher.

When the meat is done, add the peas and let them cook for another 20 minutes or until the peas are tender.

This stew can be served with noodle rice or plain rice, *m'falfal*.

Marrow Stew
Qoussa b'laban

Craving for food during pregnancy is serious business that needs attending to. Even those who dismiss it as an old wive's tale fall for the trap when they happen to be the victim. *Qoussa b'laban* was not one of my favourite dishes but when I was pregnant with my second child, I found myself constantly craving for it. The sense of wellbeing it brought on after my craving was gratified – my everfussy mother took care of that – is one of the best memories I have of this pregnancy and it is as vivid and powerful now after all these years. Needless to say, it has become quite a favourite of mine. Served with vermicelli rice, this dish warms up any heart on a cold winter day.

Ingredients

1 kg–1.2 kg (2 lb 4 oz– 2 lb 11 oz) lamb, cut up in chunks for stew
3 tbs + 1 tbs olive oil for the wok
2 tsp salt
1 tsp pepper
¾ tsp allspice
A dash of nutmeg
1,500 g (about 3 lbs) fresh marrows
4 cups sour yoghurt
4 tsp corn flour
2 tsp tomato concentrate
3 garlic cloves
2 tsp dried and crushed mint leaves

In a large pan, brown the meat in the hot oil. Add the salt and spices and enough water to cover the meat. Bring to boil then let it simmer for 60–70 minutes.

While the meat is cooking, wash and dry the marrows and cut them lengthwise once, then across so as to obtain small pieces. Add a tablespoonful of oil to a wok and stir-fry the marrows and the crushed garlic for a few minutes; cover the pan and let them cook in their juice for five minutes then add them to the meat when it is done.

In the same wok, measure the *laban* and add it to the cornflour, dissolved in four tablespoonfuls of water, and the tomato concentrate. Bring to boil while stirring the mixture gently then add to the stew. Add the crushed mint leaves to the pot and simmer for five minutes more. Serve immediately accompanied with vermicelli rice.

String Bean Stew
Yakhni fassoulia

Lamb meat is usually cooked with the bone, this goes for all stews. A favourite cut is the chest, which is carved into double cutlets, that is two ribs for every portion. When nicely trimmed, it is not as fatty as the shoulder. Some people will prefer to add ¼ tsp cinnamon and a teaspoonful of nutmeg as lamb has a much stronger flavour.

Ingredients

1 kg (2 lb 4 oz) beef or 1 kg–1.2 kg (2 lb 4 oz–2 lb 11 oz) lamb, cut up in chunks
    for stew
1 whole onion
3–4 tbs vegetable oil
2 tsp salt
1 tsp pepper
¾ tsp allspice
(You can substitute the pepper and allspice with 2 tsp of mixed spices)
800 g (2 lbs) string beans, fresh or frozen
3 tomatoes
2–3 tbs tomato paste

In a large pan, brown the meat with the onion in hot oil. Add the salt and spices and enough water to cover the meat. Bring to boil then let it simmer for 60–70 minutes. The amount of time can vary according to the type and cut of meat you use. It is to be noted that lamb cooks faster than beef, however it is always better to consult with your butcher.

Meanwhile wash the beans, then remove the strings and cut them up. Pour boiling water over the tomatoes and leave them in for a few minutes. Pare and slice the tomatoes. Add them to the pan together with the skinned and sliced tomatoes; add the tomato paste and leave on medium heat for half an hour or until the beans are well done.

This stew is best served with vermicelli rice.

Spinach Stew
Yakhnet sabanekh

Traditionally grown spinach from the south of Bethlehem, with its delicate texture and flavour, renders this dish most special. Unlike the other stews I cook, the only spice I use for this stew is pepper so as not to interfere with the subtle flavour of the spinach.

Ingredients

1 kg (2 lb 4 oz) chunks of lamb or beef for stew
1 whole onion
¼ cup olive oil
1½ tsp salt
1 tsp pepper
1.3 kg (2 lb 15 oz) spinach leaves, trimmed and washed

5 garlic cloves
1 tbs olive oil or *samneh*

In a large pan, brown the meat with the onion in the butter. Add the salt and pepper and enough water to cover the meat. Bring to the boil then let it simmer for 60–70 minutes. The amount of time can vary according to the type and cut of meat you use; in Palestinian cooking, the meat is always cooked until it is very tender.

When the meat is done, add the spinach leaves either whole or coarsely chopped. Let them cook for ten minutes.

Meanwhile fry the crushed garlic cloves in one tablespoon olive oil and add to the stew while it is cooking.

Serve with vermicelli rice and wedges of lemon on the side.

Mahashi

Mahashi dishes are associated with Sundays and holidays because they can be prepared the day before. After the family got back from church all my mother had to do was leave the prepared dish to cook while the rest of the family gathered for long drinks and appetisers.

Their preparation is elaborate and time consuming, a minor consideration in large families where many women could help. Now that the extended family has gradually given way to the nuclear family and more women are joining the workforce, these dishes have still managed to survive, thanks to the assistance of a mother, mother-in-law or generous neighbour, always eager to give a hand.

The preparation of stuffed dishes is a delicate operation requiring great dexterity and infinite patience. It requires a special coring tool that you can buy in Middle-Eastern food shops or in the Arab quarters of big cities. When I finally decided to venture into the arena of *mehshi* preparation, I reinforced my firm decision, which, by the way, elicited a great deal of scepticism, with an extravagant investment in a fancy coring tool with a beautiful wooden handle. Not a good move as it turned out, because not only did it confirm others' doubts about my initiative – I was just not the *mehshi* cook type – but it also turned out to be as useless as it looked fancy. After a few failed attempts – I broke most of the marrows and never got to the stuffing stage – I admitted defeat until my new household help offered me an offensive-looking corer that looked as if it came from a junkyard. But it worked! And it has served me all these years. I tried to tell my friends about the incredible qualities of my coring tool from the junk heap only to discover that they all had their own fancy corer at the bottom of a drawer of kitchen memorabilia and, in a top drawer, handily accessible, an exact replica of the dubious-looking instrument.

Still, the process of coring marrows or baby aubergines is a skill that will need a few attempts and a dose of will power to master. Using a knife, cut off the tip or stem of the vegetable and hold it in your left hand, with the corer in your right hand try to slowly pierce the pulp all around while pushing in the corer no more than 1 cm (½ in) at a time. Remove the loose pulp and try again in the same way, pushing the corer deeper in and removing the loose pulp until you reach the bottom. It is very important to proceed delicately against the sides of the vegetables and the bottom so as not to pierce it. If this happens, do not let it defeat you and carry on with the next one. Once you are done with the third or fourth marrow or aubergine you will get a feel for it, which will make it easier.

Stuffed Aubergines
Sheikh el-mehshi

The local variety of aubergines – the best are grown in Battir and Aroub, south of Bethlehem and are famous for their particularly pungent flavour – turn this dish into a special delicacy.

Ingredients

15 baby aubergines (makes about 1 kg/2 lb 4 oz)
½ cup olive oil

1 cup broth for the cooking
400 g (about 13 oz) *hashweh* (see recipe page 75)
30 g (1 oz) pine nuts, fried and added to the meat stuffing

Tomato sauce
6 fresh ripe tomatoes
2 tbs tomato paste
1 tsp salt
½ tsp pepper
⅓ tsp allspice
4 tbs oil (optional)

Yoghurt sauce
1½ cups broth
2 cups yoghurt
2 tsp cornflour
¾ tsp salt
½ tsp white pepper

The only way you can get this dish right is by setting aside your scruples and deep-frying the aubergines in olive oil. Wash the baby aubergines and dry them, keeping them whole with the stem so as to prevent the oil from penetrating the inside. Fry them in the hot oil until they become slightly soft to the touch. Be careful not to pierce the aubergines when you turn them over. Leave them to drain on kitchen paper while you prepare the *hashweh*, the meat and onion stuffing.

Preheat the oven to 180° C /360° F/gas mark 4 .

Remove the stems and slit an opening along the side of each aubergine away from the ends, so as to obtain a pocket, which you will fill with *hashweh*. Place the aubergines with the open end facing up in an ovenproof dish and cover with the sauce of your choice.

If you are using a tomato sauce, crush four of the tomatoes in a food processor, adding the paste and the spices and about ¾ cup water. Pour the sauce over the aubergines. Soak the remaining two tomatoes in boiling water for easy peeling, slice them and spread them evenly over the aubergines. Cover with aluminium foil and bake for half an hour. Remove the foil and check the consistency of the sauce: you might wish to add some water or some olive oil for a richer taste. Put back in the oven and bake, uncovered, ten more minutes. Serve immediately with plain or vermicelli rice.

If you are using the yoghurt dressing, it is added at the last stage of the cooking. Add one cup of broth to the aubergines and bake them, covered with aluminium foil, for half an hour. Meanwhile mix the yoghurt with the cornflour in a heavy saucepan, add half a cup broth, the salt and pepper and cook over a medium heat while stirring. Lower the heat and let simmer for five minutes.

Remove the aubergines from the oven and add the yoghurt sauce. Return to the oven and bake uncovered for another ten minutes.

Serve immediately with plain rice or vermicelli rice.

Stuffed Cabbage
Malfouf

Buying the right cabbage for stuffing is supposed to be an art, though I believe it is sheer luck. I watch as women hold a big cabbage in both hands, trying to assess the weight per volume, the same way they do with watermelons: the secret lies in the paradox that the bigger the volume the lighter it should feel. But physics have never been my forte and I rely on the choice of the greengrocer. The cabbages we use for stuffing weigh up to four kilos and are appropriate because of their wide leaves. The most flavoursome variety comes from the area south of Bethlehem and is only available in early summer, the only time of year any self-respecting cook will serve this dish at her table.

The process of preparing the cabbage is somewhat lengthy but can be done the day before. You need to buy a cabbage of at least three kilos (about seven pounds) to prepare a meal for four persons. You separate the leaves one by one until you reach the heart where the leaves become wrinkled and unsuitable for rolling, which you save for a salad.

Remove the stems from the flat leaves and cut them in squares and triangles big enough to roll into small cigars. Put a pan of water to boil, to which you add one teaspoonful of salt and cumin, and dip the leaves a few at a time for two minutes or until they are just tender enough to roll. Transfer with a perforated ladle to a colander then lay them flat on a kitchen towel to cool. Repeat this process until you have blanched all the leaves. If you stack them hot they will become too soft and will tear upon rolling. I always blanch the tender stems and use them to line the bottom of the pan. While they add extra flavour, they also protect the lower layer of *malfouf* from burning.

Ingredients

1 kg (2 lb 4 oz) blanched cabbage leaves, ready for stuffing
1 cup round grain rice
300 g (1 lb) minced beef
50 g (2 oz) butter
1 tsp *samneh* (optional)
1 tsp salt
¾ tsp pepper
½ tsp allspice
Dash of cumin, nutmeg and cinnamon

(You can substitute the spices with 1¾ tsp mixed spices)
6 garlic cloves

To prepare the stuffing, wash the rice under running water and soak it for five minutes. Drain the rice and transfer to a glass bowl. Add the meat, the softened butter, the salt and the spices and mix thoroughly.

Put the individual cabbage leaves flat on the working surface and add a heaped tablespoonful of the stuffing parallel to the veins of the leaf, roll it like a cigarette. Stack the rolls closely together at the bottom of a large pot lined with stems from the cabbage. Repeat the layers, inserting the peeled garlic cloves in between. The stacking is important as it will prevent the cabbage rolls from opening or getting too mushy during the cooking. Add two cups of hot water to the pot and cook on the stove-top on a high heat until it boils. Leave on high for five minutes – you may taste the liquid to adjust the spices if necessary – then lower the heat and let it simmer for half an hour or until most of the water is absorbed. You may want to insert an insulating griddle under the pot during the last stage of the cooking.

Serve immediately with a tomato and cucumber salad and plain sour yoghurt on the side.

Stuffed Vine Leaves and Marrows
Qoussa mehshi maʿ warak

Gone are the winter evenings where one could reminisce and drool over a plate of *mehshi u warak*, stuffed *baladi* marrows and fresh vine leaves. We had to wait for spring to get the first taste of this delicious meal! Now marrows are available all year round and vine leaves keep very well in the freezer. Still, for the most tender vine leaves it is always best to pick the first growth, preferably from the

betuni, grapevine, as it has a slightly acid flavour and does wonders in combination with the sweet marrows.

Ingredients

2 kg (4 lb 8 oz) about 16 marrows, preferably *baladi*
300 g (11 oz) grapevine leaves
2 cups round-grain rice
500 g (1 lb 2 oz) ground beef
50 g butter
1 tsp *samneh* (optional)
2 tsp salt
¾ tsp pepper
½ tsp allspice
(You can substitute the pepper and allspice with 1½ tsp mixed spices)
3 cups hot water
3 fresh tomatoes, sliced

Core the marrows to the desired thickness and leave them to soak in salted water for half an hour. Blanch the vine leaves by pouring boiling water over them in a heatproof container and soak them for ten minutes, just enough for them to get soft. Remove the marrows from the water and tip over the open end to drain properly, transfer the vine leaves to a colander and leave them to drain in the sink. The leaves tend to stick together, separate them so they drain faster.

For the stuffing you will have to wash the rice under hot running water for a few minutes then put it aside to drain. Transfer the rice to a big glass bowl to which you will add the meat, half the butter, melted, and the salt and spices. Mix thoroughly until you get an even blend of meat and rice.

You can start by stuffing the marrows. The best way not to overstuff them is to fill them until you can fit your little finger inside the marrow up to the first knuckle.

While you are sitting comfortably in front of your worktop, spread the vine leaves one at a time on the surface and put enough stuffing on the leaf to be able to roll it like a cigarette. The stuffing should be parallel to the wide end of the leaf which you will fold once over the stuffing, then flip the two ends over and continue rolling until it is tightly closed. Repeat with the other leaves, leaving a few for the bottom and top of the cooking pan.

For this amount you will need quite a large pan. It is preferable to use an old-fashioned aluminium or brass pan that diffuses the heat evenly. Cover the bottom of the pan with a few vine leaves and spread the rolled vine leaves in a circle to cover two rows at the bottom. Alternate with the stuffed marrows and finish with the rest of the vine leaves. Dot the surface with the rest of the butter and cover with a layer of sliced tomatoes. Add the hot water, cover the pot and cook over a high heat for 10 to 15 minutes. Taste the liquid to check the salt and spices, adjust them if necessary, lower the heat and let it simmer for 45 minutes or until all the liquid is absorbed. Turn off the heat and let it rest for ten minutes before serving.

If you prefer to cook this dish the traditional way, you have to substitute the beef with lamb and the butter with an equal amount of *samneh*. I prefer the healthier approach and believe that the suggested recipe above does not compromise the authenticity of the dish: the careful use of fresh spices and a small amount of *samneh* for the flavour justly restore its authenticity.

This makes the perfect Sunday dish if you prepare it one day ahead: all you have to do the next day is put it on the stove. If you are using an aluminium or brass pot, wait until just before the cooking to put the food inside.

Tips
I use an old-fashioned aluminium bowl-shaped pan without handles to cook

this dish as this allows me to flip it over in a tray for serving. The resulting display is spectacular and will certainly impress your family or your guests if you try it!

The pulp of the marrows is not to be wasted: cook over a medium heat for 15 minutes then add lemon, olive oil, salt and pepper. Or you can try the recipe for *ijjeh*.

Stuffed Vine Leaves and Marrows
Mehshi u warak siami

While many meat aficionados dismiss this dish because of the amount of time it takes to prepare – 'since you are doing it anyway you might as well add the meat,' says my husband – it is one of the finest gourmet dishes among the *mahashi*. My mother has always served it for her summer buffet dinners to the delight of all the guests, and I make sure to keep the tradition going.

Ingredients

20 marrows (about 1.5 kg/3 lb 4 oz)
200 g (7 oz) vine leaves
1½ cups rice, round grain
8 large tomatoes
1 medium onion or 100 g (4 oz) spring onions
1½ tsp salt
¾ tsp pepper
½ tsp allspice
Small bunch of fresh parsley
A handful of fresh mint leaves or 2 tbs dried and crushed mint leaves
½ cup olive oil

⅓ cup freshly squeezed lemon juice
About 2½ cups water

Prepare the marrows and vine leaves following the directions in the previous recipe.

For the stuffing, wash the tomatoes and herbs and peel and wash the onion. Finely dice five tomatoes, the onion, the parsley and fresh mint leaves and add them to the rice. Add the oil, the lemon and the spices and mix thoroughly.

Following the direction of the previous recipe, stuff the marrows and roll the vine leaves and arrange them in a medium sized cooking pot. Slice the rest of the tomatoes to cover the top, add a layer of vine leaves, add the hot water and put the pan, covered, on a high heat until it boils. Taste the liquid in order to adjust the spices and leave it to cook for 45 minutes. Lower the heat and let it simmer until all the water is absorbed. Leave to cool and sprinkle with fresh olive oil upon serving.

Serve with pickled green olives, salted black olives and a plate of *hummos*. If meat is a must, then so be it, as *kafta* is the best accompaniment.

This dish is as delicious the next day straight from the refrigerator. You can use the leftovers for a special picnic lunch or for a snack on the patio.

Stuffed Marrows with Tomato Sauce
Ablama

The traditional way requires frying the marrows after stuffing them, but I find it unnecessary and they come out just as delicious.

If you think that 30 marrows, as indicated in the recipe, is more than you need, do not hesitate to freeze some after cooking as they keep very well for at least three weeks. Such a dish as this one, which requires some elaborate preparation, is always worth doing in a large quantity. With vermicelli rice on the side, it goes a long way, and make sure to have enough sauce to moisten the rice.

You can either serve the whole quantity for a small party of friends or freeze the extra portion. One of the advantages is that it can be prepared ahead of time.

Ingredients

1 kg (2 lb 4 oz) small *baladi* marrows (about 16 pieces)
400 g (14 oz) of *hashweh*
30 g (3 oz) pine nuts
3 fresh tomatoes
1½ tbs tomato paste
1 cup water
¾ tsp salt
½ tsp pepper
⅓ tsp allspice
30 g (1 oz) butter or *samneh*

Core the marrows to the desired thickness and leave them to soak in salted water for half an hour. Meanwhile prepare the *hashweh* stuffing (see recipe page 75) adding the fried pine nuts at the very end.

Preheat the oven to 200° C/400° F/gas mark 6.

Remove the marrows from the water and let them drain upside down in a colander for a few minutes before stuffing them with the cooled *hashweh*. Stuffing them requires some patience and you have to be careful not to break the tips in the process. Line the marrows inside two greased oven pans and spread the fresh slices of tomatoes on top. Melt the tomato paste in the water to which you will add the spices, then pour over the marrows. Dot with the butter or *samneh* and bake, covered with aluminium foil, for one hour. Remove the aluminium foil, add some water if the sauce is too thick and bake, uncovered, for another ten minutes.

Serve hot with vermicelli rice on the side.

Tip

Refrigerated marrows will break upon coring. If they are not fresh from the market remove them from the refrigerator three hours ahead and core them when they are at room temperature.

Stuffed Marrows with Yoghurt Sauce
Mehshi qoussa b'laban

The advantage of this dish, like with many stuffed vegetable dishes, is that they can be prepared in advance. Traditionally this dish was prepared with *laban jmeed* or *laban immo* as it is called in the Bethlehem dialect, which has a particularly strong and acrid flavour that may not be appreciated by those who did not grow up eating it. My mother, who is not a native Palestinian, has always cooked it successfully with plain sour yoghurt. This recipe is a variation on her theme.

Ingredients

20 marrows about 1½ kg (3 lb 4 oz)
400 g (14 oz) minced beef or lamb
1 cup rice
30 g (1 oz) butter
½ tsp salt

¾ tsp pepper
½ tsp allspice

Wash the marrows and dry with a towel. Empty out their contents with a corer and let them soak in a basin of salted water for half an hour. Pour out the water and let them drain while you prepare the stuffing.

Wash the rice under the tap and let it drain in a sieve. In a glass bowl, mix the rice with the minced meat, the melted butter and the spices. Stuff the marrows one at a time pushing the stuffing inside with your little finger. In order to check if they are sufficiently full, you should be able to insert your little finger up to the top knuckle. Be careful not to over-stuff them as they will burst open during the cooking.

Put the stuffed marrows in a pan with 2½ cups broth, cover and bring to the boil over a high heat. Lower the heat and let them cook for about one hour or until they are almost done. Add the yoghurt sauce and cook for another ten minutes.

For the yoghurt sauce
2 cups yoghurt
4 garlic cloves
2 tbs cornflour
2 tbs butter or *samneh*
½ cup broth
1 tsp salt
½ tsp white pepper
Dash of freshly ground nutmeg and cinnamon

Mix the cornflour with the yoghurt and mix in the broth. In a heavy saucepan, lightly fry the crushed garlic in the butter or *samneh*, add the yoghurt mixture

Cored marrows

and the salt and pepper, heat through and add to the cooked marrows. Stir carefully so as not to break the marrows and cook on a low heat for another ten minutes. Serve very hot.

If you have any left over, refrigerate the marrows and the sauce in separate tightly covered containers, which you will put back together and re-heat in the microwave or on the stove-top.

Meat Dishes

You can spend hours in the kitchen preparing a gourmet meal, but if you do not deliver a hefty meat dish all your efforts are shrugged off as futile.

Traditional dishes that are served for formal occasions and feasts include big juicy chunks of lamb or mutton, generally served with rice. Lamb is classified by age and spring lamb, three to four months old, is slaughtered to mark special occasions when its blood is often smeared over a doorstep or a corner stone as a sign of blessing and to ward off the evil eye.

As every slaughter has more or less the character of a sacrifice, great importance is attached to the fact that the blood from a slaughtered animal shall flow over the ground so that later it may be seen that an animal has been killed.

(Karen Seger, *Portrait of a Palestinian Village,*
The photographs of Hilma Granquist)

For those who ignore such lore for more hedonistic delights, roasted spring lamb is the ultimate experience in gourmet dining.

Yearling mutton, between one and two years old is preferred by many for its stronger flavour.

Because of its tenderness and fine texture, lamb is also a favourite for barbecues. Once summer has set in, barbecues are quite the thing for less formal entertaining; indeed, from May till late September, many balconies, terraces and patios are animated with the bustle of families and friends congregating around enticing displays of *mezze* and hot grills. The best that a restaurant can offer will pale next to the array of salads and variety of meats served for a *mechoui* at home.

Lamb Chops on the Grill

Whether lamb or mutton chops, they are succulent to the last morsel over a grill fire. The following recipe can be used for the preparation of shanks of lamb cut up into cubes for the skewer or braised brisket.

Ingredients

2 kg (4 lb 8 oz) lamb cutlets, trimmed of fat
2 garlic cloves
3 tsp salt
1 tsp pepper
1½ tsp allspice
¼ cup olive oil

Mix the crushed garlic, salt, spices and olive oil and massage the mixture into the chops two to three hours before grilling.

You can serve the chops with a selection of salads, with *moussaka'a* or any vegetable dish of your choice.

Kibbeh b'suniyyeh

Lamb Kebab on the Grill

From the cafés you can smell the charcoal scent of cooking kebabs and the hot, sweet odour of Turkish coffee.

(William Dalrymple, *From the Holy Mountain*)

The best cut for lamb kebab is the loin or the leg. Ultimately however, you have to rely on your butcher who knows the quality and age of the lamb he serves best. Palestinian butchers will avoid trimming the fat from the meat and, if you are not fastidious about fat consumption, they will generously add a small piece of pure lamb fat. Another consideration is the mincing process; ideally the meat is chopped to a fine texture by hand, and as very few butchers will take the time to fulfil such a request, they will pass the meat four times through in the mincing machine, using the big-cut mould.

You will always find a restaurant to prepare *kebab* the traditional way, and the best ones are usually outside the common circuit frequented by visitors and tourists, with shabby front windows in the heart of the souks and market places.

As a health-conscious and calorie-conscious cook, I have developed my own version of preparing *kebab* by substituting olive oil for the animal fat, which gives me the exact same softness of texture and, with the right seasoning, no one has been the wiser.

Ingredients

1 kg (2 lb 4 oz) minced lamb meat, preferably trimmed of most of the fat
8 garlic cloves
¼ cup fresh chopped parsley
¾ tsp pepper

½ tsp allspice
A dash of nutmeg, cinnamon and cloves
1¾ tsp mixed spices
1 hot pepper
1½ tsp salt
50 g (2 oz) pine nuts
3 tbs olive oil

Chop the garlic and parsley in a food processor. Chop the pine nuts on a low speed for a few seconds, making sure not too crush them to a paste. Add the garlic, parsley, pine nuts, spices and the olive oil to the meat and mix the ingredients thoroughly. Shape into oblong patties around the skewers and grill for a few minutes on both sides over hot charcoals. You can alternate the *kebabs* with small onions and cherry tomatoes.

Meat and Burghol Platter
Kibbeh b'suniyyeh

A Syrian-Lebanese import, this dish has been adopted by Palestinians for generations and we have come to believe it is quite our own!

This recipe comes from my mother's kitchen and she had learned how to do it from her Syrian aunt, Marie, a star cook in the Damascus bourgeois milieu, whom I remember very vividly, particularly in relation to this dish.

She lived on the third floor of an apartment building after having moved from a large independent house in a residential area of Damascus. Every time she wanted to prepare *kibbeh* was an occasion for an emotional outburst and a great deal of flurry. She would point at an ancient looking stone trough sitting in the kitchen corner with a thick wooden pestle leaning inertly on the inside wall

and lament over how it had fallen into disuse because of 'them', and she would in turn point vigorously to the floor below. Marie recalled in endless frustration the days when she could beat the *kibbeh* at any hour of the day, at four in the morning if she chose to, without the neighbours pestering her. It had taken quite a few months and quite a few arguments before she was persuaded to invest in a manual meat chopper and, ten years later, she was still unable to come to terms with it. And when everyone gathered around the table to enjoy the *kibbeh*, she wanted continual reassurances that after all, it did come out allright, although it could have been much tastier, and one had to make do with many inconveniences these days.

Baked pan *kibbeh* is my favourite, but it can also be prepared as individual balls and deep-fried. Either way, it is not advisable to use lamb in the preparation: the shell will crumble in the pan and if you are serving *qras*, it will not be cohesive enough to hold the stuffing. You can indulge your taste for lamb in the stuffing, and your *kibbeh* will have a more interesting edge.

Ingredients

For the shell
½ kg (1 lb 2 oz) lean beef trimmed and cut in chunks for mincing
½ kg (1 lb 2 oz) fine *burghol*, cracked wheat
2 onions
2 tsp salt
¾ tsp pepper
½ tsp allspice

Wash the *burghol* and soak it in water for 15 minutes. Meanwhile peel the onions, wash them and cut them in four. Drain the *burghol* and squeeze it a handful at a time in order to get rid of the water.

Roasted leg of lamb

In a food processor, put small quantities of the meat, the *burghol* and onions and grind them to a fine pasty dough. You can add the seasoning in the process. Knead the whole lot together and set aside covered with a clean cloth.

For the stuffing
300 g (11 oz) minced lamb
1 onion
2 garlic cloves
3–4 tbs oil
¾ tsp salt
½ tsp pepper
⅓ tsp allspice
50 g (2 oz) pine nuts + 1 tbs oil

Peel the onion and garlic and chop them separately. It is possible to crush the garlic to get it really fine. In a medium-size pan fry the onion in the hot oil for three minutes stirring constantly, then add the garlic and fry till they just about start turning gold in colour. Add the meat and mix it with the onion and garlic, and fry it while stirring constantly until it turns brown. Mix in the salt and spices; cover the pan and leave to cook for another five minutes.

Heat 1 tablespoonful of oil in a small frying pan and add the pine nuts. Fry them on a low heat until they turn golden then add them to the meat. It is always wise to watch pine nuts as they can burn very quickly.

For pan *kibbeh*, divide the meat paste in two and spread half in a greased 30 cm (12 in) oven pan, making sure to spread it evenly. Spread the stuffing over the surface and cover with the rest of the paste: take a small quantity at a time and flatten it between the palms of your hands then place it over the stuffing, repeating with the rest of the paste. Spread it firmly and evenly over the whole surface up to the edges of the pan.

With a sharp knife cut through the layers in straight lines and across to form diamond shapes. Have a bowl of iced water at hand to dip the knife in to prevent it from sticking. As the meat paste is quite thick and tight, this procedure helps for even and faster cooking and will prevent the meat from getting dry. Pour a stream of oil (at least a cup) over the surface.

Put the pan in a preheated hot oven (220° C/425° F/gas mark 7) and cook, covered with aluminum foil, for half an hour. Remove the foil and cook for another ten minutes or until the edges draw away from the sides of the pan.

Serve immediately with *m'tabbal* or a salad of aubergines with yoghurt.

Kibbeh balls are the perfect finger food for a buffet dinner or a stand-up reception, and their success depends on dexterity and patience.

With your left hand take a small quantity of the meat dough – the size of an egg – and using the index of your right hand push a hole through it. Synchronise the delicate movement of your finger with the palm of your left hand to shape it into an evenly hollow oblong shell. Spoon a tablespoonful of the stuffing inside and with your thumb, index and middle finger, close it to form an oblong ball. It is very important not to press the shell on the stuffing.

Half fill a deep pan with oil and put it on a high heat then fry the *kibbeh*, no more than five at a time until they turn golden brown. Do not turn them until you are sure it is done on one side, and be careful not to pierce them or break them. Serve very hot.

Tips

After experimenting with a variety of pans, I find that an old fashion aluminum pan is best for baking.

Have a small bowl of iced water at hand in which you can dip your finger if the paste sticks to your fingers during the shaping of the balls or while you are spreading it in the pan.

To make sure that the oil is heated to desired temperature, it is the custom to fry first a small piece of bread until it turns golden brown.

Meat Shawarma

Giant *shawarma* skewers adorn the shop fronts of restaurants in every downtown area. The fast food of the Middle East, it has gained favour in many cities around the world where ethnic food is popular. Giant skewers of thin layers of lamb and fat in the shape of an inverted cone rotate in front of vertical sources of fire slowly grilling the outer layer of meat, which is gradually slivered upon demand for the passers by. It has become quite fashionable to have a *shawarma* stand installed in the garden for a party, although the cost is somewhat prohibitive. I have devised my own way for serving delicious juicy *shawarma* while cutting down on the saturated fat that comes with the commercial version. I use trimmed lamb or a nice cut from the filet of beef, which cooks quickly and remains juicy. The rest of the secret is very simple: stir-fry your meat in a wok!

Ingredients

500 g (11 lb 2 oz) beef or lamb
¾ tsp salt
½ tsp pepper
½ tsp allspice
¼ tsp each nutmeg, cloves and cinnamon
A dash of cardamom
¼ tsp gum arabic
3 tbs freshly squeezed lemon juice
¼ cup olive oil
1 small grated onion

Cut the meat in very thin long slivers and put in a glass bowl.
Pulverise the grains of gum arabic by mixing them with a dash of salt and

crushing them with a pestle and mortar. Add to the rest of the ingredients, mix well and add to the meat. Refrigerate for a few hours tightly covered till half an hour before cooking time.

Put the wok on the largest burner on high and add the meat. Fry it while stirring quickly until it is browned. Serve immediately in *kmaj* sandwiches or on a hot serving plate. Sprinkle with *tahineh* sauce and/or a mixture of slivered onions sprinkled with *sumak* and chopped parsley.

Tahineh sauce
½ cup *tahineh*
1½ tsp vinegar
3 tbs freshly squeezed lemon juice
1¼ tsp salt
⅓ tsp white pepper
⅓–½ cup water

Mix the *tahineh* with the vinegar and the lemon juice until you get a thick whitish paste. Add the water slowly and keep on stirring until you get the sauce to the desired thickness. Add the salt and pepper and serve.

Meatballs
Kafta

Kafta can be prepared with beef or mutton. It is advisable to use beef if you plan to fry them instead of baking them, or you can mix the two kinds of meat. However, there are always the purists who will only consume mutton, even for frying. It often happens that I encounter people at the butcher who will ask him to add a chunk of fat to the meat before mincing it. I personally go for beef alone and use olive oil for the fat and extra flavour.

Ingredients

1 kg (2 lb 4 oz) minced beef
6 garlic cloves
One small bunch of parsley, about half a cup, chopped
1½ tsp salt, or according to taste
½ tsp pepper
⅓ tsp allspice
A dash of cinnamon and a dash of nutmeg
½ cup vegetable oil

In a food processor, chop the garlic and parsley, then add the salt and spices and chop some more. Add to the meat in a large glass container and mix thoroughly, using a wooden spoon. Taking small quantities at a time, form into small hamburger shaped patties and set aside to fry. It is possible to refrigerate tightly covered for no more than three hours before frying them.

In a deep pan, heat the oil and fry the *kafta* a few at a time, making sure to turn them only when the lower side is totally browned. Serve immediately.

Kafta is a favourite, especially accompanied with French fries and traditional tahina salad. It is also delicious in warmed *kmaj* with a small quantity of the salad. *Kmaj* is a flat round hollow bread ideal for sandwiches with a difference: it can 'pocket' runny salads very well!

To avoid frying, it is possible to broil the *kafta* alone or with tomatoes or vine leaves. It never fails to gratify the greedy and even the less greedy.

Meatballs and Vegetables in Tahineh Sauce
Tajen

A dish that is both economical and substantial. It feeds a large family economically as a relatively small amount of *kafta* goes a long way. The following recipe is enough for six hungry adult mouths and the combination of meat, vegetables and *tahineh* make it the epitome of healthy nutrition. If you are partial to lamb, you can prepare lamb *kafta* or mix half lamb and half beef.

Ingredients

For the kafta
800 g (1 lb 14 oz) minced beef
6 garlic cloves, crushed
1 small bunch of parsley (20 g/1 oz), about half a cup chopped
1¼ tsp salt, or according to taste
½ tsp pepper
⅓ tsp allspice
A dash of cinnamon and a dash of nutmeg
(You can subsitute 1¼ tsp mixed spices instead of the above)
3 tbs vegetable oil

For the tajen
600 g (1 lb 6 oz) potatoes
500 g (1 lb 2 oz) aubergines (about one large *rihawi* type)
500 g (1 lb 2 oz) marrows
4–5 medium tomatoes (about 500 g/1 lb 2 oz)
1 medium onion (about 100 g/4 oz)

For the sauce
¾ cup *tahineh*
¼ cup freshly squeezed lemon juice
1½ cups water

Prepare the *kafta* by mixing the meat, the crushed garlic, the chopped parsley, the spices and oil and shaping the mixture into round or oblong patties (about 20 patties). Set aside.

Soak the tomatoes in boiling water for a few minutes to make them easier to peel. Wash, peel and cut the vegetables, including the tomatoes, into coarse cubes. Slice the onion into thin slivers and add to the vegetables. Season with the salt and spices and transfer to a large oven-proof pan. Add the *kafta* at regular intervals, cover with an aluminium foil and bake in a preheated oven (220° C/ 425° F/gas mark 7) for one hour.

Meanwhile prepare the *tahineh* sauce by mixing the *tahineh* with the lemon juice and the water until you get a smooth runny sauce. Cook in a saucepan over low heat on the stove for a few minutes while stirring constantly. Let it simmer for three to four minutes then add to the cooked meat and vegetables mixing it thoroughly with the juices. Bake another 15 minutes in the oven uncovered and serve very hot.

Serve it accompanied by a simple green salad, many families serve it with plain or vermicelli rice.

Minced Meat rolled in Vine Leaves
Kafta u warak dawali

Kafta mixture (see above)
20–25 vine leaves, preferably *betouni*

2 tomatoes
½ cup olive oil

Prepare the *kafta* as indicated in the recipe above, mixing in half the quantity of oil. Taking a small quantity at a time, shape into thick short cigars, 2 cm (1 in) in diametre and five cm (2 in) long; set them aside while you prepare the vine leaves.

Wash the vine leaves and put them in a deep stainless steel container; pour boiling water on them until they are covered. Leave them to soak for five minutes then let them drain for a few minutes. In a similar way leave the tomatoes for a few minutes in boiling water, then remove the skin and set them aside.

Using a wooden board or a worktop spread the vine leaves one at a time with the larger end towards you, put one *kafta* on that end and close the leaf around it starting with the sides and rolling towards the other end. Put the rolled *kafta* in a greased oven pan.

Once you have finished, slice the tomatoes and place them over the *kafta*; sprinkle with a dash of salt and the rest of the olive oil. Bake in a hot oven (250/450/gas mark 8) for 40–50 minutes.

This dish can be served with a variety of steamed vegetables or French fries. For a more special meal, add a plate of the *tahineh* salad.

Minced Meat with Onions
Hashweh

800 g (1 lb 14 oz) minced beef or a mixture of half beef, half mutton
3 onions
8 garlic cloves
¼ cup olive oil
1½–2 tsp salt

1 tsp pepper
1½ tsp mixture
80 g pine nuts (3 oz) + 1 tbs olive oil

Peel the onions and garlic and chop them separately. It is possible to crush the garlic to get it really fine. In a medium-size pan heat the oil and add the onions, fry them for a few minutes on a high heat stirring constantly and when they become soft add the garlic. Keep on stirring until the onions and garlic just start turning golden then add the meat and mix thoroughly. Brown the meat and make sure to stir it often so it does not stick. If you think it is necessary, add a small amount of oil. When the meat is totally browned, mix in the salt and spices, cover the pan and leave to cook for 10 to 15 minutes or until all liquid from the meat evaporates.

Heat 1 tablespoonful of oil in a small frying pan and add the pine nuts. Fry them on low heat until they turn golden then add them to the meat. Pine nuts are very tricky and can burn very quickly, that is why it is always safer to fry them separately and on low heat.

This *hashweh* can add an interesting dimension to a plain omelette or to *hummous*. Added to *moussaka'a*, it becomes a dish worthy of a special occasion. It is a basic stuffing for many vegetable dishes as well as for *sambousek*, pastry stuffed with meat or cheese.

Pot Roast

I learnt how to make a pot roast Armenian style from a soft-spoken elegant lady who lives in a suburb of Jerusalem. It is thanks to her that I learnt to cook some of the Armenian recipes in this book. As I sit with Shoshana Hagopian on her front verandah, quietly sipping tea and delicately nibbling on a scrumptious home-made chocolate cake, she repeats to me for the umpteenth time how Armenians will always keep their nationalistic spirit, no matter where they are or where they go. Still, she regrets that so many have left Jerusalem and so many young ones are seriously considering leaving, especially for the United States where so many of their kin are well established.

Ingredients

1.5 kg (3 lbs 4 oz) beef for pot roast
2 carrots, peeled and cut into thin sticks
6 garlic cloves, whole
1 tsp salt
1 tsp pepper
1 large onion, whole
60–80 g (about 3 oz) Butter
1 cup red wine

Insert the blade of a knife in two or three places on both ends of the meat, sticking it in deep enough to allow the carrot sticks inside. Season the carrots with salt and pepper and insert the sticks in the deep holes, together with the garlic.

In a heavy pan, melt the butter on a high heat and fry the meat till it is browned on all sides. Add the onion, some salt and pepper to taste, and a cup of dry red table wine. Bring to the boil uncovered and leave to cook until reduced by half. Add enough hot water to cover and simmer for one hour, depending on the cut and the way you like it done.

Serve with *plaki* and fresh steamed vegetables and a green salad on the side.

Roasted Leg of Lamb
Fakhd kharouf bel Furun

A yearling makes this dish both special and quite extravagant and it therefore needs a special occasion. I cooked it for French cousins from Burgundy, great connoisseurs of food and wine who were visiting Bethlehem while I was working on this book, and they were so delighted with the dish that they had seconds and smothered the accompanying rice with the sauce.

Ingredients

A leg of lamb of about 2.5 kg (5–6 lb)
4 garlic cloves
A handful of rosemary leaves
2 tsp salt
2 tsp spice mixture
½ cup olive oil (80 ml)

Preheat oven to 240° C /475° F/gas mark 9.

Put the leg of lamb, largely trimmed of its fat, into an oven-proof tray and put in the very hot oven to sear for half an hour, turning it over once.

Meanwhile put the garlic, rosemary, salt, spices and olive oil into the food processor and mix at high speed for one minute. When the meat is seared, baste it with the mixture on one side and put it back in the oven, which you lower to 220° C/425° F/mark 7, repeating the process 15 minutes later. After another 15 minutes, turn the meat over and baste the other side twice at 15 minutes intervals. Cover the meat with foil paper and let it cook for another hour. Transfer the meat to a serving dish and the sauce into a bowl and serve immediately with plain rice and steamed vegetables.

Poultry

As late as the early sixties barter was still a common practice even among the townsfolk who saw a remarkable influx of villagers on a daily basis. Even a practising paediatrician like my father had to be part of this network, to my mother's total dismay. How many times did a grateful patient leave a live chicken on his desk for services rendered! What ensued was a flurried chicken chase and a flutter of feathers after which the sweaty maidservant, adept at such manoeuvres, would carry the perplexed bird to the neighbour across the street who, like a good Muslim, slaughtered the animals according to the ritual procedures of *halal*. For many years I believed that chicken, rabbits, lambs, and such gifts as my father received by way of remuneration, belonged to the Muslim faith. To add confusion to ignorance, our maidservant, not especially noted for being clever, convinced me that our neighbour had lost his leg because the ghosts of the dead chicken had picked at it for so many nights that he had been left with only one leg and that he would soon lose the other if the neighbourhood kept turning to him for this serial slaughtering.

However, that was not quite the end of my trials in the realm of winged creatures! Ever since my early beginnings as a shy cook, I had resolved to handle only the freshest produce that the surrounding farms could offer and stay away from the comfortable pitfalls of frozen foods and pre-packaged fare. My mother's influence and my subscription to an exclusive cooking magazine compounded my efforts. So I headed for the market-place to buy a fresh chicken!

There were endless rows of cages with noisy chickens bickering at the shoppers and at each other, but hard as I looked, nothing that looked close to anything that could go in the oven was to be seen. One vendor invited me to pick any bird I fancied. He then picked up a fowl, demonstrated with a grand gesture that it was the choicest in the brood, and without giving me the chance to respond, he expertly twisted its neck while mumbling the formula of *halal*. Revolted by this unexpected spectacle, I turned round and left the market-place, postponing such expeditions to an undetermined future date.

Chicken in the Broiler
Djaj bel-furun

2 fat chickens
2 lemons, cut in four
2 tsp salt
2 onions
6 garlic cloves
¼ cup oil
Salt and pepper to taste
A few whole grains of allspice

Cut the legs and breasts of each chicken, setting aside what is left of the chicken for broth or for soup. Sprinkle the pieces with salt and pepper to taste and rub lightly with the oil of your choice. Set them in an oven pan.

Peel the onions, then wash them and cut them in four; peel the garlic cloves and keep them whole. Add them to the chicken tray and put the tray in a pre-heated oven to 250°C/450°F/gas mark 8 for one hour or until they are well cooked and the skin is golden. Serve immediately.

This chicken goes very well with potatoes and rosemary. It is also a perfect supplement to a plate of oriental rice. If you wish to serve it with the rice, especially at a buffet dinner, it is advisable to remove the skin and bones from the cooked chicken, cut the meat in slivers and spread it over the rice. Put on top a generous amount of fried almonds and pine nuts and serve immediately.

Chicken on a Skewer
Shish taou'

1.5 kg (3 lbs 4 oz) of chicken breasts cut into big bite-size pieces
1½ tsp salt
¾ tsp white pepper
½ tsp allspice
1½ tbs *sumak*
5 garlic cloves, crushed
2 tbs fresh lemon juice

Cut chicken breasts into big bite-size cubes and add salt, pepper, allspice, *sumak*, crushed garlic and fresh lemon juice. Mix well so as to distribute seasonings on all the chicken and refrigerate tightly covered for two hours.

When you put the chicken on the skewer, make sure there is enough space between the pieces to allow for even grilling without having to overcook them. You might need eight minutes for each side. Serve immediately.

Any leftover chicken you might have will do very well the next day as a cold meal. Spread some olive oil on half a *kmaj* or a roll, grill it slightly in the toaster oven and add the cold chicken. Serve a salad with it, and you will have a feast!

Chicken Shawarma

While lamb is a staple of *shawarma*, chicken has recently made a major break-through and has become quite a favourite. My butcher confided in me that while chicken is increasingly popular, shopkeepers still add layers of lamb fat in between the layers of chicken to guarantee a full flavour!

My response to such stratagems is home made *shawarma*, juiciness and flavour guaranteed!

Ingredients

600 g (1 lb 6 oz) breasts of chicken
1 tsp salt
¾ tsp pepper
¾ tsp allspice
¼ tsp each cinnamon, nutmeg, cloves and cardamom
(2 tsp spice mixture)
¼ tsp gum arabic
¼ cup olive oil
3 tbs freshly squeezed lemon juice.

Measure the olive oil and lemon juice into a bowl. Prepare the spice mixture: grind the cinnamon, cloves and cardamom and grate the nutmeg, measure them and add to the oil and lemon. Crush the gum arabic with the salt to a fine powder and add it to the mixture. Mix and pour over the whole chicken breasts and marinate overnight in the refrigerator in a tightly covered container. The next day you will need 40 minutes for preparing and serving.

Drain the chicken breasts from the marinade and fry in a heavy saucepan on high heat, turn them over and once they are browned lower the heat and cover the pan; let them cook for a few minutes. Transfer the chicken to a wooden board and cut the pieces across into thin slivers. Serve with a *tahineh* salad or serve individual portions of the chicken in pocket *kmaj* breads – four to six sandwiches – to which you add *tahineh* sauce and slivered onions sprinkled with *sumak* and some chopped parsley.

Chicken with Rosemary

One large chicken, cut in eight pieces
⅓ cup olive oil
1 onion, whole
2 twigs of rosemary
1 tsp salt
¾ tsp white pepper
4–6 grains of allspice
1 cup chicken stock

Measure the olive oil in a deep pan and fry the skinned chicken pieces a few at a time, turning each piece once as it browns to a light golden colour. It is healthier to have the skin of the chicken removed, however this is a matter of taste and choice. Remove the chicken from the oil and place it on kitchen paper to absorb the extra oil.

Transfer the chicken to a heavy pan and add the rest of the ingredients. Put in a pre-heated hot oven (220° C/425° F/gas mark 7) for one hour or on top of a stove on high heat until it boils, then lower the heat and leave it for about an hour or until the chicken is tender.

It is possible to add a few potatoes half an hour through the cooking time. Peel and cut the potatoes the way you like them and just add them to the pan. If you pre-fry the potatoes, 15 minutes cooking time will be sufficient after you add them to the chicken. I like to use a cast iron pan or an earthenware pan for this particular dish. Make sure, however, that the latter can go on a stove-top, otherwise bake the dish in the oven.

Chicken with Onions and Sumak
M'sakhan

M'sakhan comes from the Tul-Karem and Jinin areas north of Bethlehem. As a speciality, it certainly competes with *mansaf* and *kiddreh* as the representative Palestinian dish. It is one of the dishes at which many restaurants excel. The secret of its success is in the bread, which should be neither too thick nor too thin. The *tabun* is the famous clay oven that was a centrepiece in every garden or backyard *hakura*, a small plot of land. When this bread is not available, it is possible to use *kmaj* bread, which is thick enough to carry the stuffing.

M'sakhan is a favourite at informal family gatherings where everyone should forget about using a fork and knife and dig in with the hands. One of my most vivid childhood memories is a Friday we spent with friends, wealthy landowners of proud peasant stock, who lived in a big mansion in Tul Karem. The host was a real patrician, proud to be surrounded by his large family and his equally large wife who wore her beautifully embroidered *thawb* with a great deal of dignity and grace. She had tattoos on her forehead and chin and underneath her stately headwear, her thick braids were dyed with henna.

The house and garden teamed with grown-ups and children of different ages, and babies were handed over from the wet nurses to the mothers, the aunts or the guests, and some would burst out crying, utterly confused by the number of unfamiliar faces.

Needless to say, the star of the day was the *m'sakhan,* served in huge copper trays on bread, just as it came out of the *tabun*. While the men consumed large quantities of the delicious meal under the trellis in the garden, the women sat in the cool of the big dining room and teased the pregnant women about the magic of *m'sakhan* for pregnancy. There must have been at least three pregnant women present and by the end of the day, everyone swore to the fact that *m'sakhan* does indeed induce easy delivery.

Later on, all the women retired to the many bedrooms especially setup for a general post-luncheon siesta. A scream broke the stillness of the slow afternoon, upsetting the shadowy light that had just settled on the marble floors of the cooling bedrooms and creating commotion among the bevy of half-naked women. In an instant, the whole house was in uproar as one of the women, very pregnant but not due until a month later, broke her waters and went into labour. Half the household accompanied her to the hospital and two hours later a young boy came running down the dusty street announcing the addition of another boy to the family.

That day it was agreed that *m'sakhan* was indeed a harbinger of happy news!

There are three stages for cooking this dish and the preparation is not complicated if the instructions are followed carefully. Do not hesitate to use your own recipe for preparing chicken broth and broiling the chicken, provided it does not call for more than the standard ingredients. The key ingredient is the *sumak*, which you buy as whole grains unless you have a really reliable *'attar*, or spice vendor. It is common practice for sellers of spices to camouflage adulterated *sumak* with colouring.

Indeed, the key to the success of this dish is in the timing.

Ingredients

For the chicken
2 chickens from the farmer's market

1 onion, peeled and cut into eight pieces
4–6 garlic cloves
Salt and pepper to taste

Cut out the legs and breasts of the chicken, setting aside what is left, necks and wings, for the broth. Season them with the salt and pepper and spread them in a greased oven tray.

Add the onion pieces and garlic and put in a preheated oven for one hour or until they become golden and tender.

For the broth
Remaining parts of the chicken, necks and wings
3 cups water
1 small onion, whole
2 garlic cloves
4–6 grains allspice
1 small cinnamon stick
1 slice of lemon
Salt and pepper to taste

Put the necks and wings in a pot and cover with water, approximately three cups. Add the rest of the ingredients and bring to the boil on a high heat. Lower the heat to medium and let it simmer for 30–40 minutes. Add water if necessary in order to have at least two cups of broth at the end of the process. Strain the broth in a container and set aside.

This broth can be prepared ahead and refrigerated in a well-sealed jar as this will save you time. Avoid using commercial broth, which might contain preservatives or spices incompatible with this dish.

For the stuffing
6 medium sized onions, about 1 kg (2 lbs 4 oz)
2 tsp salt
1 tsp pepper
½ tsp allspice
3 tbs *sumak*
2 cups broth
1 cup extra quality olive oil

Peel and finely chop the onions and put in a casserole. Add the salt and cook covered over a low heat until the onions become transparent and soft, about half an hour. Add the spices, the broth and the oil and bring to the boil. (The stuffing can be prepared a few hours ahead.)

Cook for five minutes more and the sauce is ready for serving

For serving
6–8 hot *tabun* breads
¼ cup *sumak*
80 g (3 oz) pine nuts

Now that the chicken and stuffing are ready, spread the hot bread on a big serving plate, a traditional brass *sidir* is ideal for this kind of dish. Add at least ¾ cup stuffing to every piece of bread, add one piece of chicken on top. Cover the chicken with some more of the stuffing and sprinkle with pine nuts.

Sprinkle the portions with more *sumak* and the plate is ready for the enjoyment of your family or your friends! My youngest daughter, Maha, a student in Paris, holds regular M'sakhan evenings for her French and Middle Eastern friends.

Tip
Formerly bread arrived at the table straight from the *tabun*. The best way to heat the *tabun* bread is to wrap it with foil paper and put it in the hot oven for 8=−10 minutes.

Grilled Chicken
Djaj meshwi 'al fahem

Chicken barbecued on coal is quite an adventure if you can get it crisp and juicy. It is quite a favourite exercise for Friday or Sunday luncheons, any time of the year except on the few days when it rains, and for summer dinners on the terrace or under the trellis.

I always tend to buy chicken legs, a first choice among members of my family. You can also use the breasts, which can be equally juicy thanks to the marinade. One important tip is to keep the skin on through the cooking and leave the option of removing it to individual taste.

Ingredients

8 legs of chicken
1¼ tsp salt
¾ tsp white pepper
4 garlic cloves crushed
1 hot pepper very finely chopped
¼ cup lemon juice
¼ cup olive oil
A small handful of fresh thyme leaves or 1 tbs dried and crushed thyme

Rinse the legs and tap them dry with a paper towel. Prepare the marinade with the rest of the ingredients and add it to the chicken and refrigerate for at least three hours in a tightly covered container. Remove from the refrigerator half an hour before grilling time as it is always better to have them at room temperature for cooking.

Sear them on very hot coals on both sides, turning them over once, then close the lid of your grill and cook them slowly for 45 minutes or until they are done to your liking. You have to check them regularly to make sure that they cook evenly; you might have to turn them once.

If you have an open grill, sear them on both sides then baste them regularly with the marinade, turning them over once, until they are done.

Serve immediately with baked potatoes or French fries and a traditional salad.

Stuffed Chicken
Djaj mehshi

Easy to prepare, chicken stuffed with meat, rice and pine nuts is a festive dish and its success depends greatly on the clever use of fresh spices. In preparing this dish, you have to count one stuffed chicken per four persons.

Ingredients

1 large chicken (about 1.5 kilos/3 lbs 7 oz)
1½ tsp salt
1 tsp white pepper
1 tsp freshly grated nutmeg

For the stuffing
1 tbs butter
150 g (5 oz) ground lean beef
¾ tsp salt
⅓ tsp pepper
½ tsp allspice
½ tsp nutmeg
⅓ tsp cinnamon
(or 1½ tsp mixed spices with an extra dash of nutmeg and cinnamon)
½ cup regular grain rice
30 g (1 oz) fried pine nuts

Rub the chicken with the two halves of a lemon and set it aside for half an hour, after which rinse it under the tap and leave it in a colander to drain. Just before stuffing it, rub the inside with salt and nutmeg and sprinkle salt and white pepper on the outside.

Meanwhile brown the ground beef in the butter on a high heat, stirring occasionally, until all the liquid from the meat is absorbed. Add the salt and spices and stir. Wash and drain the rice and add it to the pan, stirring until it is mixed with the meat. Measure out ¾ cup hot water and add to the rice mixture. Cover and bring to the boil, then lower the heat and cook for five minutes before turning off the heat. Add the fried pine nuts and then spoon the mixture inside the chicken. Secure the end with toothpicks or by sewing the skin together. Put the chicken on a greased pan and cover with aluminium foil. Cook in a preheated oven (220° C/425° F/gas mark 7) for about an hour. Uncover and cook 15 minutes more until the chicken turns golden. You might need to spoon out some of the juices on the chicken. Serve immediately.

You can serve with extra *hashweh* rice and an assortment of steamed vegetables. A bowl of sour yoghurt can be included.

Tip
The rice should be less than half cooked when the stuffing is spooned inside the chicken.

Bread and Dough

At one end of the courtyard was the quarter's communal bread oven, (*tabun*). This small conical structure was made from stone rubble, and roofed either by a stone vault or wooden beams. Inside, there was a circular mud case, known as 'the house of bread' (*beit al-'aysh*), which was placed over a shallow fuel pit. This case was approximately 70–80 cm in diametre at the base, tapering to an open top of about 40 cm, and was built by women from a local yellow clay (*huwwar*) mixed with straw.

The oven was heated with sticks and crushed olive pits. Once the fuel was glowing, it was topped with small, smooth pebbles. The open top case was then covered by a tin sheet with a handle, and dried dung and other slow-burning materials were put around the mud hearth for additional heat. Once the proper temperature was obtained, soft dough cakes were placed over the hot non-stick pebbles and baked.

The *tabun* played an important role for the village women, who would sit inside its cramped interior telling jokes and exchanging news while their bread baked. The *tabun* therefore functioned for women as the guest-house (*madafeh*) did for men.

(Suad Amiry and Vera Tamari, *The Palestinian Village Home*)

Bread Topped with Meat
Sfiha

Sfiha is a favourite in day to day family cooking and can be carried in a lunch box to school or to the office. It serves very well as finger food for a party or buffet dinner. Many believe that the success of *sfiha* lies in the dough, however a failed stuffing can spoil even the best of dough. In the Bethlehem area, *tahina* is an important component of the stuffing, which, combined with vinegar, gives it an interesting combination of nutty and acid flavours.

In the average Palestinian household, no less than a hundred *sfiha* are prepared at once to serve the midday meal, for extra snacks and to send at least two dozen to the closest or favourite neighbour. It is an affront to have the smell of baking emanating from one's house and not share the end result.

Ingredients

For the dough
500 g (1 lb 2 oz) white flour
1 tsp instant active dry yeast
1 tsp salt
⅔ cup olive oil
1 cup sour yoghurt (200 g/7 oz)
¾ cup warm water

For the stuffing
400 g (14 oz) minced beef
2 medium fresh ripe tomatoes
1 medium onion
3 garlic cloves

1 hot pepper
1¼ tsp salt
½ tsp pepper
½ tsp allspice
⅓ cup *tahineh*
2 tbs white vinegar

Measure and sieve the dough in a large container, mix in the salt and the yeast and add the oil. Mix together and then add the yoghurt, mixing some more with your hands. Add the water a small quantity at a time all the while working the dough by pressing with the heels of your hands, folding and turning; repeat the process until you obtain a smooth elastic texture. Shape the dough into a ball and leave in a warm place for two hours or so.

Mince the tomato, onion, garlic and hot pepper in a food processor and add to the meat together with the salt, pepper and allspice. In a small bowl, mix the *tahineh* with the vinegar until you obtain a thick smooth paste. You might need to add a tablespoonful of water if the paste is too thick. Fold in this mixture with the meat.

When the dough has risen to almost double its size, punch it down and divide it into two balls. Leave it to rest for another half-hour. Taking one portion at a time, roll out the dough onto a floured surface to about 1 cm thickness (½ in) and using a cutter (6–8 cm/2½–3 in diametre) cut circles into the dough. Remove the edges of dough and shape into a ball and leave to rest for later use. Put the circles of dough onto a greased baking sheet some 2 cm (1 in) apart and spoon out a generous portion of stuffing onto each, flattening it with the back of a spoon. Repeat the same process with the rest of the dough.

Put to bake in a preheated oven at 230° C/450° F/gas mark 8 for about half an hour. Remove from sheet and let cool on a grid. Serve with a plain lettuce salad or with sour yoghurt.

This recipe makes about 35 *sfiha*.

Cheese Kisses
Sambousek b'jibneh

The ideal finger food for receptions and a special accompaniment to pre-dinner cocktails. The word *sambousek* derives from the root *bassa*, meaning he kissed; I chose to translate it into kisses. Many homes and caterers prepare cheese *sambousek* with ready-made French pastry dough, practical enough and quite tasty, but not quite the real thing especially if you are serving it with an assortment of *mezze*.

Ingredients

For the dough
400 g (14 oz) white flour
¾ tsp instant dry active yeast
1½ tsp salt
150 g (6 oz) soft butter
1¼–1½ cups warm water

For the stuffing
320 g (12 oz) semi-salted white sheep-cheese
1 egg
A small handful of fresh thyme leaves or 1 tbs dried and crushed thyme

Measure the flour, yeast and salt and mix in the butter, working it slowly in the flour. Add warm water, small amounts at a time and work in the dough, pressing with the heels of your hands and turning until you get a soft malleable dough that is not sticky and that is easy to spread with a rolling-pin. Shape into a ball and cover, and set aside in a warm place for two hours or until the dough is double in size.

Prepare the thyme leaves by removing them from the stem and washing them under the tap. Lay aside to dry on a kitchen towel.

Meanwhile grate the cheese or, if it is soft enough, mash it with a fork. Add the scrambled egg and thyme and mix.

When the dough is ready, punch it down and divide it in two. Spread one half with a rolling-pin on your clean worktop and, using a cutter – between 5 and 7 cm (2 to 3 in) depending on how small you want your *sambousek* – cut circles into the dough. Pick up one circle, fill it with the cheese mixture and fold one half over the other. You can seal the edge by pressing the tip of a fork against the sides or by twisting it with the thumb and index finger starting from one end of the folded half circle to the other end. Place the *sambousek* on a greased baking sheet 3 cm (1¼ in) apart and leave to rest for 20 minutes before baking in a very hot oven (230° C/450° F/gas mark 8) for half an hour or until the *sambousek* are baked golden. Serve hot, warm or cool.

Have the heart to try them fried and they are unforgettable.

This recipe makes about 40 *sambousek*, using a 7 cm (3 in) cutter.

Tip

You can use parsley or basil instead of thyme, to which you may add ¼ cup of finely chopped black olives. It is up to you to experiment and find out what is most agreeable to your taste.

Cheese Pie
Sou beurek

The trick in this recipe is in the preparation of the dough. The portions have to be rolled out into very thin sheets and boiled in water, one sheet at a time, for seven to eight minutes, then dipped in cold water for a few seconds and laid out on a clean kitchen sheet to dry. While dexterity is required, patience is essential in the success of this dish which is a must at every Armenian gathering.

Ingredients

For the pastry
4 cup flour
4 eggs
½ tsp salt
About 500 g (1 lb 2 oz) slightly salted sheep cheese for the stuffing
200 g (7 oz) soft butter

Sift the flour with the salt into a bowl, make a well in the middle and add the slightly beaten eggs. Mix the two ingredients slowly and knead the dough until it becomes smooth and soft. You might need to add some flour if you think it is too sticky, however, be sure to add just a small amount at a time in order to obtain the right texture and softness.

Divide the dough into ten small portions shaped into balls and leave to rest for one hour covered with a damp cloth.

On a floured surface, roll out each ball into a very thin sheet 35 cm in diametre, which is the size of the tray you will need. Setting two sheets of dough aside, cook the remaining eight in the boiling water as indicated above, one at a time and dipping each sheet in the cold water to interrupt the cooking process. Lay them carefully on the sheet to dry.

Spread one of the uncooked sheets on the greased tray and brush with butter. Add four layers of cooked dough, each time spreading the surface with the butter. Lay the cheese in thin slices over the surface and continue layering with the four cooked sheets, always alternating with butter. Lay the remaining uncooked sheet on top and again brush generously with butter.

Cook for 40 minutes in a preheated moderately hot oven (190° C/375° F/gas mark 5), or until the surface turns golden and the bottom is crisp. Cut into diamonds and serve immediately.

Lent Cakes
Farayek b'zeit

Members of the Orthodox community are stricter about observing the Lenten fast than any other Christian community in Palestine. The only sweet they allow themselves is the famous *farayek b'zeit*, sweet buns flavoured with the unique aroma of *mahlab*. This recipe makes about 15 cakes.

Ingredients

500 g (1 lb 2 oz) white wheat flour
¾ tsp salt
150 g (5 oz) sugar
1½ tsp *mahlab*
1 tsp instant active dry yeast
¾ cup corn oil
¾ cup warm water

Measure and sieve the dough in a large container, mix in the salt, the sugar, the powdered *mahlab* and the yeast and add the oil. Mix together with your fingers until the oil is totally absorbed. Add the water a small quantity at a time all the while working the dough by pressing with the heels of your hands, folding and turning; repeat the process until you obtain a smooth elastic texture of very soft consistency. Shape the dough into small balls and flatten them out on a greased oven tray a few centimetres apart. Leave the cakes to rest covered with a clean kitchen towel until they have doubled in size. Bake in a hot oven (230° C/450° F/ gas mark 8) for half an hour.

For extra special *farayek*, sprinkle them with sesame seeds and brush them with egg whites beaten with a tablespoonful of water.

Meat Kisses
Sambousek b'lahmeh

The same as cheese *sambousek*, those with meat are ideal as finger food for a party, in a *mezze* or part of an *hors-d'œuvres* platter. The dough is crustier and, if you can forego with health scruples and calorie counting, they are most delicious fried.

Ingredients

For the dough
400 g (14 oz) white flour
¾ tsp instant dry active yeast
1¼ tsp salt
50 g (2 oz) soft butter
¼ cup olive oil
2 egg yolks
About 1 cup water

For the hashweh
400 g (14 oz) minced lean beef
1 large onion

4 garlic cloves
¼ cup olive oil
1 tsp salt
1 tsp pepper
¾ tsp allspice
(1 tsp mixture)
40 g pine nuts (2 oz) + 1 tbs olive oil

Measure the flour, yeast and salt, make a well in the centre and add the butter, the oil and the egg yolks. Work the ingredients gradually into the flour. Add warm water small amounts at a time and work in the dough, pressing with the heels of your hands and turning until you get a soft dough with a fine texture that is easy to spread with a rolling-pin. Shape into a ball and cover, and set aside in a warm place for two hours or until the dough has doubled in size.

Meanwhile peel the onions and garlic and chop them separately. It is possible to crush the garlic to get it really fine. In a medium-size pan heat the oil, add the chopped onion, and fry for a few minutes on high heat stirring constantly. Add the garlic and fry some more then add the meat and mix thoroughly. Keep on stirring the meat until it is evenly browned then mix in the salt and spices, turn it around two or three times and remove from heat.

Heat one tablespoonful of oil in a small frying pan and add the pine nuts. Fry them on a low heat until they turn golden then add them to the meat.

When the dough is ready, punch it down and divide it in two. Spread one half with a rolling-pin on your clean work table and, using a cutter – about 6 cm (2 in) depending on how small you want your *sambousek* – cut circles into the dough. Pick up one circle fill it with one heaped teaspoon of the cooled meat stuffing and fold one half over the other. You can seal the edge by pressing the tip of a fork against the sides or by twisting it with the thumb and index finger starting from one end of the semi-circle to the other. Place the *sambousek* on a greased baking sheet 3 cm (1½ in) apart and leave to rest for 20 minutes before baking in a very hot oven (230° C/450° F/gas mark 8) for half an hour or until the *sambousek* are baked golden. Serve with a *tahineh* salad, tomato salad or with *mafghoussa*.

The above recipe makes about 70 *sambousek*.

Spinach Breads
Qras b'sbanekh

For the dough
1 kg (2 lb 4 oz) white flour
½ cup olive oil
2 eggs
1 level tbs salt
1 tbs instant active dry yeast
2½–3 cups warm water

Pour the flour in a large glass container add the salt and mix. Make a well in the centre, add the oil and the beaten eggs and mix thoroughly.

Add half a cup of the water to the leavening and leave to rest for a few minutes. Add to the flour mixture and knead until all the water is absorbed. Add more water and knead some more, pressing with the heel of your hand and turning until you get a soft uniform dough that is easy to roll. You have to keep in mind that the dough should be firm enough to hold the spinach mixture.

Divide the dough into three balls, cover and set aside until they double in size.

For the stuffing
1 kg (2 lb 4 oz) fresh spinach
200 g (7 oz) spring onions or 2 medium onions
2 tsp salt
4 tbs *sumak*
½ tsp pepper
1 cup olive oil
⅓ cup lemon juice

The preparation of the stuffing will need approximately half an hour. For best results, it is advisable that you proceed with it just before the dough is ready in order to avoid it getting soggy. It is also important to drain the spinach leaves thoroughly upon washing, that is why you can start by washing them and letting them drain on a clean kitchen towel.

Wash the onions and chop finely. Add the salt, pepper, *sumak* and oil and mix thoroughly. Set aside.

On a clean wooden board, chop the spinach and place in a glass bowl to which you will add the onion dressing. Mix very well. The stuffing will be reduced to almost half.

Grease three oven trays and have them handy for the spinach 'pockets'. Turn the oven on 230°C/450°F/gas mark 8.

On a clean worktop, sprinkle some flour; take one portion of dough, place it on the floured area and roll out carefully, making sure not to stretch the dough. The dough should be just thick enough to hold the stuffing without tearing. Divide it into circles about 6 cm in diametre. Put a piece of the dough flat on your hand and spoon some of the stuffing on top. Starting from the edge while using the thumb and index finger, seal the dough until you reach the centre. Do the same with the remaining two sides until you obtain a pocket with a triangular shape. Place on the tray. The first two or three attempts might prove difficult at first but the process of forming the triangular pockets will become easier as you go on.

Let the first tray rest for half an hour before you place in the oven. Proceed with the rest of the trays in the same manner. Baking time is about half an hour, depending on whether you prefer them more or less crisp. Leave to cool on a grid and enjoy!

Tips

When you are embarking on such a project, call your friends to share the work with you; they will be more than happy to take home a few *qras* in return.

This recipe yields about 70 spinach breads. You can have more if you want bite-size pieces that will look really elegant at a reception or as an accompaniment for cocktails.

Spinach pockets freeze very well. All you have to do is defrost them four hours ahead at room temperature and put them to warm in a preheated oven for five minutes. No one can tell the difference!

Thyme Bread
Qras b'za'tar

Qras b'za'tar can be served as a variety with other breads such as *kmaj, tannur, saj* or *shrak,* as it is sometimes called, and they are very similar to the foccacia served in Italian restaurants. They make a healthy snack for children to take to school. My daughter Maya enjoys experimenting with this recipe by alternately using rosemary, garlic, onions or cardamom with repeated success.

For the onion version, use a small chopped onion for the same amount of flour, fry it lightly in one tablespoonful of olive oil and add to the dough with the prescribed amount of olive oil. To prepare cardamom bread use green cardamom that you roast lightly in a heavy pan and crush with a pestle and mortar just before using. As cardamom has a powerful slightly bitter taste with a hint of camphor flavour to it, it is enough to add one teaspoonful of both the husk and grains with the flour, at least for your first try.

Ingredients

600 g (1 lb 6 oz) white flour
1½ tsp salt
1 tsp instant dry active yeast
½ cup fresh thyme leaves or 2 tbs dried crushed thyme
1 cup olive oil
1½–1¾ cups warm water

Measure the flour, yeast, salt and thyme in a deep bowl and mix in the oil, working it slowly in the flour mixture. Add the water small amounts at a time and work in the dough, kneading and turning, until you get a soft malleable dough that is not sticky and easy to spread. Shape into a ball and cover, and set it aside for one hour or until the dough has doubled in size.

When the dough is ready, punch it down and divide it in two. Spread one half with a rolling-pin about 1 cm thick on your clean worktop and, using a 7 cm cutter (3 in) cut circles into the dough and put on an ungreased baking sheet and leave to rest for 20 minutes. Bake in a hot oven (230° C/450° F/gas mark 8) for half an hour. Let cool and serve immediately to accompany salads. You get about 2½ dozen *qras*.

Sweets and Desserts

Having crossed the hill, we entered the rich vale of Shechem, or Nablus, clad with olives, full of gardens and orange groves with palm trees and watered by plenteous rills.

(H.B. Tristram, *A Journal of Travels in Palestine*)

Nablus owes its particularities to its geography and the developments of its more recent history. Its situation naturally marked it as the centre of an ancient road system and the many springs that fed the wadis blessed the area with groves and rich vegetation.

All central Palestine could be taken in at a glance, and the lesson of geography could not be easily forgotten.

(H.B. Tristram, *A Journal of Travels in Palestine*)

The view from Mount Gerizim, highest peak overlooking the central regions with Nablus sprawling the valley and the steep slopes to the north and south, justifies its nomination as 'the uncrowned queen of Palestine'. Nablus's happy location in the mouth of the only east-west path makes it the natural capital of the mountain region. Its past as an urban settlement goes back to 4500 BC and its current name derives from Flavia Neapolis, a Roman colony established in 72 AD on the site of present day Nablus.

In the seventeenth century, during Ottoman rule, Nablus headed the *liwa'* of two hundred villages and was affiliated to the Damascus province. The administrative reforms of 1887–88 and the establishment of *mutassarifiyat,* governorates, resulted in linking the *mutassarifiyah* of Nablus to the *wilayet* of Beirut, while the autonomous *mutassarifiya* of Jerusalem dealt directly with Constantinople. These new administrative divisions contributed to remarkable differences in the social development of the Nablus area and, more particularly, promoted its specificity as a culinary centre.

Nablus is especially renowned for its sweets, and *knafeh*, the emblem of a long-standing tradition of Palestinian sweet-making originated there.

One of the main ingredients used in the preparation of many desserts is white sheep's cheese, a cheese that is typical of Palestine where there is no cheese culture per se. Its processing has remained unchanged through generations. It was processed in spring when pastures are green and the milk is bountiful and was cooked and preserved in salted water for year-round consumption. Although dairy plants have been supplying the market with the same type of traditional cheese, many households continue the practice of boiling and preserving their own cheese for the year, and others still depend on their traditional supplier from Nablus.

The essential components in the preparation of this cheese are *izha, mahlab* and gum arabic that are added in the cooking process. The cheese is then preserved in large glass jars or large tin containers and is desalinated in small batches according to consumption by soaking it for a few hours in water. For the preparation of desserts, it has to be totally desalinated and needs to be soaked at least overnight.

A friend of my mother's, Nihaya, originally from Nablus, taught me how to prepare some of the desserts included in this section. The desserts she serves at her dinner parties have earned her quite a reputation in Bethlehem circles, where she has been living for 30 years.

Aniseed Rings
Baskot yansoun

Occasionally my mother used to buy tin cans of English assorted biscuits and she would save the cans for later use. I remember these cans vividly with the pictures of the Tower of London, Buckingham Palace and other London landmarks on the sides, portrayed against brilliant blue skies. What I remember most is their recycled use as they lined the upper shelf of the kitchen sideboard and held within their shiny interior the most delicious homemade biscuits in the world. It was a comforting presence that speeded up many a tedious homework and inspired rare accomplishments of dexterity on the pianoforte: I still recall with almost Proustian vividness the pleasure of soaking a well-earned reward in a cup of sweet tea with hot milk. It seems to me that my childhood days must have drifted through the heady aroma of baking that clung to the walls and the furniture, until the challenge of later years when I struggled to join the anorexic ranks of the post Twiggy generation!

Aniseed biscuits will always be a teatime favourite. While the original recipe calls for clarified butter, it comes out equally delicious with regular butter. This recipe yields about 2½ dozen biscuits.

Ingredients

2 cups flour
½ cup sugar
100 g (4 oz) clarified butter

1 egg
⅓ tsp aniseed and caraway mixture

Preheat the oven to 200° C/400° F/gas mark 6.

In a glass bowl, measure the sifted flour, and add a teaspoonful of baking powder and the aniseed and caraway mixture, the sugar, butter and egg and mix thoroughly. Divide the dough in six balls and on your worktop roll out each into a ¾ in rope. Cut it at 6 cm intervals and form each piece into a small circle. Place on a greased baking sheet. Bake for 30 minutes until they turn slightly brown. Let them rest for three minutes before moving them to a cooling rack. Serve immediately or store in a jar or tin can.

Apricots in Syrup
M'rabba mishmish

My father's generation feasted on dried raisins, apricots, figs or dates accompanied by almonds and walnuts. While fresh apricots, especially *mishmish mistkawi* from the Beit-Jala area, were a favourite, the next best way to enjoy them was as a preserve in syrup. The key to this recipe is not to overcook the apricots in order to finish the cooking process in the sunshine.

Ingredients

1 kg (2 lb 4 oz) apricots
2 cups water
½ kg (1 lb 2 oz) sugar
1 tbs freshly squeezed lemon juice
½ cup whole blanched almonds

In a pan, mix together the sugar and the water and put to boil on medium heat. Wash and dry the apricots and drop them a few at a time in the syrup, bring them to the boil and cook them for four minutes. Remove them to a tray and repeat the process until all the apricots are cooked. Add the lemon juice and let the syrup boil for another ten minutes until it starts to thicken. Turn off the heat and set it aside to cool. Open the apricots slightly from the top, remove the stone and add an almond. Put them back in the tray and pour over the cooled syrup to cover them completely. Set them covered with a thin cloth in direct sunlight, on a windowsill or on the ledge of the terrace for a few hours for three days. Preserve in a sterilised airtight jar and store away from heat.

You can serve this dessert with vanilla ice cream or *m'hallabiyeh*.

Armenian Helva

A traditional Armenian dessert from the old country, it is served on special occasions. Easy to prepare, it is preferable to serve it fresh and warm.

Ingredients

3 cups semolina
200 g (7 oz) soft butter
50 g (2 oz) pine nuts
1½ cups sugar
1 cup milk
1 cup water

Melt the butter in a heavy saucepan and add the semolina and pine nuts mixing thoroughly. Keep on stirring the mixture on medium heat until the pine nuts turn golden. Turn off the heat.

In another saucepan, measure the sugar and mix in the milk and the water and bring to boil over medium heat. Add to the hot semolina while stirring efficiently and bring to boil once more. Remove from heat and leave to rest for one hour. Mix and serve in individual plates, sprinkled with a dash of cinnamon.

Butter Biscuits
Ghraybeh

Before cream puffs, pies and éclairs became standard fare, every christening, circumcision or wedding was an occasion to offer *ghraybeh*. Just like Scottish shortcake, they melt in the mouth and disappear in a jiffy. Make sure not to overeat!

Ingredients

120 g (4 oz) clarified butter
50 g (2 oz) or ½ cup icing sugar
2½–2¾ cup flour
1 tbs *arak*

Beat the butter and sugar with a mixer until it becomes creamy. Add the arak and gradually add two cups of the flour while beating constantly. Gently knead the thick batter adding flour in very small quantities at a time until it just stops being sticky when you roll it between the palms of your hands. Taking small quantities of batter, roll into an S or shape into small flat circles which you should hollow with your index finger.

Bake in a preheated moderately slow oven (170° C/325° F/gas mark 4) for 20 minutes until they are dry but before they brown. *Ghraybeh* biscuits have to be pearl white. Makes 2½ dozen biscuits.

Cheese Dessert
Knafeh

This speciality of Nablus is the most representative Palestinian dessert. A delicacy, it is served at banquets and special receptions.

One basic ingredient is vermicelli dough, only obtainable in certain stores or at better suppliers of Middle-Eastern food. The other is the cheese, which is more readily available. I have experimented with this dessert by using fresh mozzarella and have alternated with using it ever since.

The easier way to prepare the dough is with a steamer, cooking small quantities at a time for ten minutes. The other method requires care and patience: cook small quantities at a time over very low heat by turning over the loosened dough with your fingertips. Either way, the tricky part is the final cooking as you cannot bake *knafeh* in the oven.

Ingredients

1 kg (2 lb 4 oz) vermicelli dough
600 g (1 lb 6 oz) soft unsalted sheep's cheese
½–¾ cup soft butter (you can add to it 1–2 tsp *samneh*)
1 tsp orange food dye, special for *knafeh* (optional)

For the syrup
4 cups sugar
1¾ cups water
2 tbs lemon juice

Use fresh sheep's cheese or soak your preserved cheese overnight, changing the water at least once. Either way, put the cheese on kitchen paper to get rid of the excess water and either grate it or squash it with a fork. If you are using fresh mozzarella, drain properly and slice it into thin slices. Set the cheese aside until the dough is ready.

Prepare a round baking tray with shallow edges – 46 cm (18 in) in diametre for the quantity of dough indicated in the recipe – by mixing two tablespoonfuls of butter with the dye and generously greasing the tray.

If you choose the steaming method, add ½ cup butter to the dough as you finish and mix gently. The other method also requires you to 'grill' small quantities at a time in a tray over a very low heat. Divide the butter and the dough, at least into four portions for one kilogram, and for every portion melt the butter and mix it thoroughly with the dough. Put the tray over a very low heat and turn the dough around with your fingertips until it just about starts to change in colour. Be sure not to overcook or you will end up with a dry dessert. Remove from heat. Repeat with the rest of the dough in the same way, each time adding butter and mixing it thoroughly with the dough.

Spread two thirds of the dough evenly to cover the bottom of the greased tray and press it with the palm of your hands, particularly round the edges, until it becomes compact. Spread the cheese over the layer of dough to cover it entirely and press it gently with the flat of your hand. Cover the cheese with the rest of the cooked vermicelli dough and press lightly with the palms of your hands. Cover with a large sheet of aluminium foil.

The second stage of cooking is a delicate procedure requiring no more than half an hour. Sweet speciality shops until very recently in Nablus cooked the *knafeh* on a traditional wood fire, they now use gas stoves with wide burners especially designed to spread the heat all around the tray while holding it a few centimetres above the burner. As stove-tops are not designed for this purpose, I use two grid diffusers under the tray and rotate it at eight-minute intervals, making sure that the centre does not overcook. Once all the edges pull away from the tray, it is an indication that the cooking is done. Turn off the heat.

M'tabbaq

While the tray is slowly simmering dissolve the sugar in the water in a casserole and bring to the boil. Let it boil for a few minutes then add the lemon juice and let it boil for another three minutes.

When the *knafeh* is ready, remove from heat and flip over into another, slightly bigger tray. Pour the syrup over the whole surface and decorate with coarsely chopped pistachios and serve immediately. Leftover *knafeh* can be heated in a double boiler or in the microwave oven, tightly covered at medium power.

Cream Pudding with Pistachios
'Eish es-saraya

'*Eish* means bread. '*Eish es-saraya*, literally 'the bread of the palaces', is an appellation laden with images of a thousand and one dreams and totally appropriate to this delectable dessert. This layered dessert can turn any dinner party into an unforgettable experience.

Kishta is a double cream of thick consistency that can be bought from Middle-Eastern pastry shops or supermarkets. A good substitute is double cream or fresh cream.

Ingredients

½ loaf of sliced white bread (250 g/9 oz), grilled
2 cups water
1½ cups sugar
1 tbs freshly squeezed lemon juice
1 tsp rose water
350 g (12 oz) *kishta*

1 cup milk
1½ tbs cornflour
2 tbs rose water
80 g (3 oz) shelled and chopped pistachios

Chop the grilled bread in a food processor on low so as to get coarse but small chunks. Spread the crumbs at the bottom of a rectangular medium size serving plate – about 25 cm (10 in) – with a 6 cm (about 2½ in) edge. To prepare the syrup, dissolve the sugar in the water and let it boil for a few minutes, adding the lemon juice in the process. Add the rose water after you remove it from the heat. Pour it hot over the bread so as to soak it completely. With the back of a fork, press the layer of sweetened bread against the bottom of the plate so as to form an even, thick layer.

In a small casserole, mix the *kishta*, the milk and cornflour thoroughly and bring to the boil on a medium heat, stirring constantly with a wooden spoon. Cook over a low heat for a few minutes or until the cream pudding is thick enough to cling to the back of the spoon. Remove from the heat and add the rose water. Spread the pudding over the bread mixture covering it completely. Sprinkle a thick layer of pistachios on top and let cool. Refrigerate for a few hours before serving.

If you are using fresh cream, add three tablespoonfuls of cornflour to three cups of fresh cream and cook the same way as *kishta* adding the rose water last.

Date Cakes
Ka'k b'ajweh

Date cakes are traditionally shaped like rings and symbolise the crown of thorns put on the head of Jesus at his crucifixion. Traditionally prepared for Easter, many families will not serve them at any other time of year. They are invariably served with *ma'moul*, made with the same dough but with a walnut or pistachio stuffing.

Towards the end of Lent women get together in each other's houses to share in the preparation of these cakes. They catch up on the latest town gossip while their hands get busy in the chain: one kneads, the other gets the date stuffing ready and the third stuffs while a fourth does the carving.

Even women with large families who are working have not renounced this tradition and will organise their evenings around this self-imposed task. Some of them will supplement their income and make the cakes for less assiduous women who have relinquished this habit.

Ingredients

500 g (1 lb 2 oz) fine wheat semolina
200 g (7 oz) clarified butter
1 tbp *samneh* (optional)
½ cup *sirej*, sesame oil
½ tbs active yeast
4 tbs sugar
1½ tbs orange blossom essence

For the stuffing
150 g (5 oz) thick date paste
¼ cup soft butter
½ tsp freshly ground cinnamon

The dough mixture needs to rest for a few hours or overnight: melt the butter (and the *samneh)* and work it delicately into the semolina. Add the *sirej* and mix thoroughly until all the fat is absorbed into the semolina. Leave to rest covered for a few hours or overnight.

When it is time to prepare the cakes, add the yeast, dissolved in three tablespoonfuls of water, and the sugar and the essence, and knead the dough adding warm water a little bit at a time until you obtain a soft, smooth mixture. Working the dough is very important and determines the success of your baking. Leave the dough to rest for two hours before shaping the cakes.

Knead the date paste with the butter and cinnamon and shape into ropes ¾ cm in diametre. Have a small plate of flour handy to dip your fingertips in if the paste gets too sticky.

Take a quantity of dough the size of a ping-pong ball, and spread it on your worktop into an oblong flat strip. Add a small portion of the rolled out date paste and wrap the dough around it to cover it completely. Shape the cake into a ring and, resting it on the palm of your hand, pinch a grooved design all over the surface using special picking tweezers. Place on an ungreased baking sheet and leave to rest for one hour.

Bake in a moderately hot oven (190°C/375°F/gas mark 5) for 25–30 minutes. (Makes about 15 cakes).

Filo Dough with Cheese
M'tabbaq

The options for the stuffing make this sweet dish quite versatile: it makes a wonderful dessert for a festive dinner, concludes a light brunch on a high note and adds a traditional touch to an afternoon tea.

The basic filo dough is available in most shops that specialise in Middle-Eastern or Greek food and in the better supermarkets. In the Nablus area, where this dessert is called *kellaj*, the filo dough is made with fine semolina as opposed to flour, which gives the dessert a lighter texture, however regular filo will do as well.

Ingredients

500 g (1 lb 2 oz) ultra thin filo dough
150 g (5 oz) soft butter
600 g (1 lb 6 oz) soft white sheep's cheese, unsalted

For the syrup
2 cups sugar
1½ cups water
1 tbs lemon juice
1 small cinnamon stick

By soaking the cheese overnight you remove all the salt, unless it is fresh. Grate or mash the cheese with a fork, whichever is easier and set it aside while you prepare the dough.

Heat the oven to 210° C/410° F/gas mark 6.

Grease a large tray 45 cm in diametre with 5 cm edges or a square 45 cm tray. Spread a filo sheet and brush it all over with butter. Add another sheet and repeat the same process until you have five sheets evenly stacked. Spread the cheese over the surface, brush it with butter and top with the remaining five sheets, brushing each in turn with butter, especially the top layer. With a sharp knife cut the surface into squares letting the knife almost reach the bottom.

Put in the oven to bake; it takes approximately 45 minutes to bake and for the surface to become golden and crisp.

While the *m'tabbaq* is baking, dissolve the sugar in a cup of water in a casserole, add a small cinnamon stick and put it on medium heat. Once it boils add a tsp of lemon juice and let it boil for eight to ten minutes.

Pour over the *m'tabbaq* the minute you take it out of the oven and leave to rest for a few minutes. Cut the pieces and serve hot or warm in individual plates. You can sprinkle some crushed pistachios on every portion.

Walnut stuffing
200 g (7 oz) walnuts, crushed
50 g (2 oz) sugar
1 tsp cinnamon
2–3 tbs butter

Mix the walnuts with the sugar and cinnamon and spread them over the layers of filo dough as the above. Dot with the butter. Cover with more layers of filo, cut in diamond shapes and bake in the same way.

You can use four apples, peeled and sliced, to which you will add three tablespoonfuls of honey and ½ teaspoonful of cinnamon.

Fritters with Syrup
Zalabiyeh

The poor man's dessert, *zalabiyeh* are fried and served immediately sprinkled with icing sugar or syrup. In Nablus, they are traditionally served for breakfast with *halawet el-qaryeh*, a thick and sweet pumpkin preserve. I love *zalabiyeh* with azarole jelly; the day my mother cooked this jelly she always treated us to the fritters that we dipped in the first batch of barely cooled jelly.

Any leftover dough will do, however the traditional way is the simple basic dough of flour and water.

Ingredients

> 2 cups flour
> Dash of salt
> ¾–1 cup warm water

Measure the flour and add the salt. Pour in half a cup of warm water and mix the dough thoroughly; add another quarter cup of water and work the dough by pressing the heels of your hands in the dough, folding and turning; repeat the process adding a few drops of water until you obtain a smooth, elastic, soft dough. Shape the dough into a ball and leave to set in a warm place for one hour.

Sprinkle the worktop and the dough with flour and roll out the dough in a thin sheet. Cut it out into small triangles. Sprinkle them with black cumin seeds or habet el-baraka and fry them in hot oil. Serve immediately.

Fruit Salad

I went down in the garden of nuts, to see the green plants of the valley, to see whether the vine budded, and the pomegranates were in flower.

(*Song of Songs*)

This version of fresh fruit salad owes its success to the velvet smooth sauce made with *qamardin,* and the contrast with crunchy walnuts.

Qamardin is a sweet made of apricot paste. It is available at most Middle-Eastern food stores in the shape of candy sheets.

The fruits suggested above may be substituted with any of your choice or according to what is available in the market. I always include bananas and apples as basics. I prefer to use the more flavourful *baladi* apples from the Battir and Beit-Ummar areas during summer when they are in season. Alternate peaches with kiwis, pineapples or mangoes and add pomegranates whenever they are available.

Ingredients

4 apples
3 peaches
2 bananas
1 pomegranate
½ cup coarsely chopped walnuts
½ cup raisins (optional)
100 g (4 oz) *qamardin*
¾ cup water
¼ cup freshly squeezed lemon juice
¼ cup freshly squeezed orange juice
2 tbs rosewater

Soak the *qamardin* in ¾ cup of water for one to two hours or until it is completely dissolved. The resulting sauce should have the consistency of molasses. Add ¼ cup each lemon and orange juice and two tablespoonfuls of rosewater and set aside while you cut up the fruits. You can add the sauce to the salad one hour before serving and chill in a tightly covered container.

Add the chopped walnuts just before serving.

Tip
Raisins are a nice addition for a winter fruit salad. Add them just before serving.

Pudding with Pistachios
M'hallabiyeh

Serve it warm in winter and chilled in summer.
The following recipe makes four servings.

Ingredients

4 cups milk
8 tsp cornflour
½ cup sugar
1½ tbs rose water
½ tsp gum arabic (optional)

Heat three cups of the milk. Mix the cornflour in the remaining milk and stir until it dissolves. Add the hot milk while stirring and cook on a medium heat while stirring constantly. When it starts to bubble, lower the heat and cook for a few more minutes until the mixture clings to the back of the wooden spoon. Remove from heat and pour into individual bowls. When it has cooled serve sprinkled with crushed pistachios.

Rice and Milk Pudding
Haytaliyieh

I stayed home with my mother and grandmother and watched my mother cook a dish she had promised me: *haytaliyeh*, a rice and milk pudding. The milkwoman had knocked at our door, and my mother had bought a few pints of milk from her, which the milkwoman had poured into the cooking pot. This was an important event because my mother used to say she could not afford to buy milk except on special occasions and when absolutely necessary.

No sooner was I alone than I looked at the white appetising dish with burning desire. I stretched out my finger to it and tasted it. How delicious it was!

I let my friends in, and together we pushed open the big iron door of our house and entered. There were seven or eight of us.

In spite of the darkness, the rice-and-milk pudding on the floor was glowing like the sun. I dragged it to a spot near the door for more light, and said, 'Sit down.'

(Jabra Ibrahim Jabra, *The First Well*)

Ingredients

4 cups milk
4 tbs powdered rice
4 tbs sugar
2 tsp rose water

For the garnish
Blanched and lightly roasted almonds, crushed
Lightly roasted pine nuts
Freshly grated coconut

In a heavy casserole dissolve the rice in one cup of the milk and gradually add the rest of the hot milk, stirring constantly with a wooden spoon in order to avoid lumps from forming. Cook over a medium heat while stirring patiently as it might take a good 20 minutes. When it starts boiling reduce the heat to low and cook for another few minutes or until the pudding covers the back of the wooden spoon. Add the sugar and rose water and stir some more then turn off the heat. Serve immediately in individual bowls. You can eat it warm or cold from the refrigerator. Garnish each bowl with the almonds, pine nuts and coconut just before serving.

Semolina Cake
Harissa

Harissa is yet another poor man's dessert but is quite a favourite among all my four children. Nancy, an older aunt of the family, used to visit us frequently, always bringing with her a tray of *harissa*. She would insert an almond in one of the pieces as an unusual gift. My eldest daughter, Mona, always keen to get the gift herself, would gorge herself on the *harissa* and force me to intervene discreetly with the aunt, begging her to slip the piece on her plate.

Now that they are all grown up and studying abroad, they still expect her to visit with her speciality whenever they come for the holidays.

If you are a determined fan of *samneh,* you can add one or two teaspoons to the syrup for the flavour, but remember to reduce the amount of butter indicated in the recipe.

Ingredients

3½ cups semolina
1 cup sugar
2½ cups yoghurt
½ tsp sodium bicarbonate + ½ tsp water
Blanched almonds or pine nuts for decoration

Syrup
2 cups sugar
1 cup water
100 g (4 oz) butter

Heat the oven to 180° C/360° F/gas mark 4.

In a glass bowl, mix the semolina, sugar, yoghurt and dissolved bicarbonate and pour the mixture in a greased 30 × 25 cm (12 x 10 in) cake pan. Decorate with the blanched and halved almonds or the pine nuts and put in the hot oven.

Meanwhile dissolve the sugar in the water in a casserole and on a medium heat until it boils. Turn off the heat and add the butter. Stir until it dissolves.

Pour the syrup over the *harissa* the moment you get it out of the oven. Serve warm.

Stuffed Semolina Pancakes
Qatayef

Once the month of *Ramadan* begins every bakery and every other shop sets up a stand to prepare *qatayef* for the numerous shoppers, who stop and indulge in this irresistible temptation, no matter how overloaded with shopping bags. The *iftar*, the meal served after sunset to break the fast, announced officially after the evening prayer in every city, town and village all over Palestine, cannot be complete without the *qatayef*.

In the Bethlehem and Jerusalem areas they are traditionally prepared with semolina, however, in Nablus and the Galilee, most probably due to Syrian influence, they are also prepared with a flour batter. Either way, they are quite popular and can be prepared with a variety of stuffings and in different sizes, depending on the occasion. Small bite-size *qatayef* are quite a sensation in large receptions and for special occasions.

Ingredients

3½ cups fine semolina
½ tsp salt
1 tsp active yeast dissolved in 3 tbs water
1½–2 cups water

Walnut stuffing
500 g (1 lb 2 oz) chopped walnuts
1 tsp cinnamon
½ cup sugar

Cheese stuffing
600 g (1 lb 6 oz) white sheep's cheese, unsalted
½ cup sugar
1 tsp orange blossom water

Mix all the ingredients in a glass container, adding enough water to obtain a medium thin pancake batter. Cover it and leave it to rest for at least one hour. Once you are sure that the leavening has occurred, whisk the batter and pour small quantities at a time on a greased and hot cast-iron skillet. Remove from heat when bubbles appear on the surface and place on a clean towel over a *tabak* or wicker tray.

Prepare the stuffing of your choice. Mix the crushed walnuts with the cinnamon and the sugar; or mash the white cheese to which you add some sugar and mix. Experiment by substituting cottage cheese. It really works.

To stuff the *qatayef,* place the pancake in the palm of one hand and spoon a small amount of stuffing in the centre, flip one side over the other and stick the edges together using the index and thumb. The final product has the shape of a crescent. Place the *qatayef* on a greased pan, dotting each with ½ tsp of butter and bake in a preheated oven at 180° C/ 360° F/gas mark 4 for 20 minutes. Make sure you do not overbake as the edges will become quite dry and tough to chew.

Prepare the syrup with three cups of sugar dissolved in 1¾ cups of water, to which you add two teaspoons of lemon juice. Pour over the *qatayef* the moment you get them out of the oven. Serve immediately.

Tips
When you prepare the pancakes, have a small cup of oil at hand in which you dip kitchen paper in order to grease the skillet after each pancake.

Once the pancakes are ready you have to stuff them immediately otherwise they will not close properly. Stuffed *qatayef* can be refrigerated for up to two days. Bake them and add the syrup for immediate consumption.

Tamriyeh

A specialty from the Nablus area, this delicacy is most commonly served for breakfast. Instead of using the regular syrup I like to serve it with azarole jelly. It is essential that this dessert be served immediately after frying.

The following measurements are enough for 15 fingers.

Ingredients

See recipe for *zalabiyeh*

For the stuffing
1½ cups semolina
1 cup milk
½ cup sugar

Turn over the semolina in a greased saucepan on a low heat for eight minutes. Add the sugar and milk and stir, cooking the mixture for another five minutes until it pulls away from the sides of the pan. Spread it on a lightly greased square or rectangular plate or on a greased foil paper until it cools, then cut it into small rectangles 3 x 1 cm (1 in x .).

Spread the dough onto a floured surface and cut it into rectangles big enough to wrap around the semolina fingers. Press both ends with a fork and fry in hot oil. Serve immediately with a syrup or jelly of your choice.

Walnut Cakes
Ma'moul

Ma'moul always accompanies the date cakes, *ka'k b'ajweh*, as an Easter sweet and the same dough is used. It symbolises the sponge that was used to wipe the face of Jesus as he suffered on the cross. As is the case with the date cakes, 'pinching' the finished cakes with special tweezers is an exercise in patience and creativity that not many women enjoy. It is delicate but necessary work as it allows the cakes to hold the powdered sugar with which they are sprinkled before serving. It is customary to stuff these cakes with walnuts, although pistachios have become quite popular, especially in the Nablus and Galilee areas.

On a lighter note, Anton Shammas, a Palestinian writer from the village of Fassuta in upper Galilee has this story to tell about walnuts.

Fifty walnuts were arranged in a line on the upper ledge of the house, and Grandfather Jubran, from where he stood on the lower level, had to crack them with blows from his forehead. The nuts cracked open one after the

Ma'moul

other, but the heart of the employer's daughter was harder to crack, and he did not win her heart.

(Anton Shammas, *Arabesque*)

Ingredients

For the stuffing
200 g (7 oz) walnuts
1 cup sugar
½ tsp cinnamon

Take a small quantity of the dough and roll it into a ball about the size of a ping-pong ball. With your index work an opening in the dough and keep on widening the opening and thinning the sides until you obtain a pocket in which you spoon a small amount of stuffing. With dexterity and some delicacy, close the opening and flip the small cake over and, with a light touch of the fingers, shape it into a small dome. While still in your palm, take the tweezers and lightly pinch the whole upper surface of the cake. Place on a tray and repeat. This recipe makes about 15 cakes.

Wheat Pudding
Burbara

Marakat kameh, which literally translates as wheat pudding, is the old appellation for this spicy pudding that is more commonly referred to as *burbara,* after Saint Barbara whose feast falls on 4 December.

In Beit-Jala, a town that borders Bethlehem, it is customary to serve the strained wheat for funerals. Among the Armenian community this dessert, called *Anush abur*, is served for Christmas. It is often garnished with pomegranate seeds instead of the raisins.

Preferably served hot, this highly flavoursome pudding warms up the heart as the cold settles in seriously for the winter season. The key to successful *burbara* pudding is in the spices, it makes a big difference if you use freshly grilled seeds and grind them on the spot. To grill the fennel and aniseed seeds, put a small frying pan over a low heat, and when it is hot, add the required amount of seeds and stir for a few minutes.

Ingredients

250 g (9 oz) wheat
1 cup sugar
2 tsp cinnamon
2 tsp aniseed
2 tsp crushed fennel seeds

60 g (2 oz) each
Blanched almonds
Pine nuts
Chopped pistachios
Chopped walnuts
Raisins

Measure the wheat in a large pan and cover with two litres of water. Cook until the wheat doubles in size. You might need to add some more water during the cooking. Add the spices and sugar and stir until the sugar dissolves. Lower the heat and cook for another few minutes. The consistency of the pudding should be creamy.

Serve hot in individual bowls and garnish according to taste.

Jams

While jams have become readily available in supermarkets and grocery stores, nothing replaces the unique flavour of home-made apricot jam, or quince and azarole jellies, the three classics in my repertoire and traditionally Palestinian.

Apricot Jam
Tatli mishmish

Beit-Jala apricots are regionally famous for their special aroma and sweet flavour. It is the fruit which emigrants from the Bethlehem area miss the most. They have ascribed to it such qualities that 'eat *mishmish mistkawi* and die' is not an overstated expression of their longing for this fruit. In their memory, it has come to embody everything good that the earth can provide and the pride that Beit-Jala people take in this ambrosial delicacy is reflected in the price they charge. The whole Bethlehem area all the way south to Hebron cultivates this apricot but cultivators in Beit-Jala will always consider their product of superior quality and flavour.

The buzz around a season's harvest starts at the onset of the month of May when prospective buyers start canvassing the orchards as to who has the biggest and sweetest fruits for the best price. Many drive south to the villages to pick the fruits themselves at a special price.

When it comes to the jams, the secret lies in getting it just the right colour. Indeed, the lighter it is the more praise is due. I remember as a child when my mother boiled the jam in a big pot, her anxiety as she checked the consistency and watched for the right moment when she could remove it from the fire. She then poured it in big trays that she covered with snow-white thin fabric and laid out on the terrace in the full sun. For four to five days we were forbidden from playing on that terrace so as not to disturb the rows of trays with the luscious jam basking in full sun from morning until dusk. My mother has always prided herself in making the lightest jam in the whole of Bethlehem and her secret was simple: the cooking process was completed outdoors in full sunshine!

I remember in previous years when I cooked 8 *ratls* (24 kg) of apricots and distributed them to family and friends.

This recipe is enough to make 12 175 g (6 oz) jars.

Ingredients

3 kg (6 lb 8 oz) fresh apricots
1.8 kg (4 lb) or 8 cups sugar
Juice of 1 lemon

The basic quantity of fruits for the preparation of jams is three kilos, which is equivalent to one *ratl*, a minimum weight measure in large families.

Wash and dry the apricots on a clean kitchen towel. Cut them in half, removing the stone and put them in a large deep pan. Measure the sugar and add to the apricots stirring very well with a big wooden spoon until they are thoroughly mixed. The mixture should not fill more than half the pan as it might overflow on boiling.

Put the pan on medium heat and stir constantly until the sugar melts. At this first stage of the cooking it is important to make sure that the sugar does not form any crystal lumps. Once the sugar has thoroughly melted, increase the heat and bring to boil – it takes between 10 to 15 minutes – but be careful not to let it overflow. Cook uncovered for an hour, skimming the foam that accumulates on the surface. Add the lemon juice five minutes before removing from the heat.

The traditional way of preserving the jam was to let it cool thoroughly before putting it in the jar then pouring hot wax over the surface in order to seal the contents. It is now possible to find sealing jars in speciality shops. I pour out the jam in the jars while it is very hot and seal them immediately.

There are two ways of finding out when the jam is done: if the jam separates upon stirring, revealing the bottom of the pan, it is a sign to proceed to the second test. Spoon out a very small quantity of the jam on a glass plate and put it in the refrigerator for a few minutes to cool; this will allow you to test the consistency and decide whether you should remove it from the heat or cook it some more.

Your undivided attention is necessary in the last stage of the cooking, as it will determine the successful outcome of your endeavour. If you want to try the 'sun technique', do it with a small quantity of jam the first time. Measure a small quantity in a glass pan when the jam is just starting to have body – about 45 minutes after it has started to boil – and set the pan out in full sun covered with a light cheesecloth for a few hours, every day for three days. The resulting jam will be lighter and tastier! Your success should give you enough confidence to go ahead with a whole batch the next time. At a time when commercial jams were not as available as they are today, an average family cooked some 15 kilos of apricots for the whole year. Nothing has changed today; as any commercial apricot jam is an understatement compared to home made *tatli mishmish mistkawi*!

Azarole Jelly
Tatli za'rur

The season for cooking quince and azarole jellies coincides with the bustle of the olive harvest and the many tasks associated with the preparation of olives for pickling and for the press. The best azaroles grow wild on bushes that can reach two metres. Local lore would have it that when the olives are abundant, azarole bushes yield poorly and vice versa.

Azarole jelly can be used instead of honey or syrup to sweeten *tamriyeh* or *zalabiyeh*. A spoonful of it in hot milk is supposed to clear the nastiest throat. I love to serve it with vanilla ice cream.

Ingredients

3 kg (6 lb 8 oz) azaroles
6 cups sugar
Juice of 1 lemon

Wash the fruit under running water. As they are small, the biggest the size of a large olive, they are cooked whole. Put them in a pan and cover them with water. Make sure that the fruit is covered with water and cook it covered on a high heat until the azaroles are soft and you can mash them with the back of a spoon. It takes about one hour. Allow it to cool for one hour then pour out the contents through a fine sieve lined with cheesecloth into another pan.

Measure the sugar, add to the pan and put it back on a high heat. Cook uncovered for 40 minutes skimming the foam whenever it appears on the surface. At this point start checking the consistency by spooning a small amount on a small plate and letting it cool in the refrigerator for two minutes. When the sample rolls slowly on the plate without dripping it is an indication that the jelly is ready. Remove from heat and transfer to sterilised jars that you close immediately. Makes about seven 175 g (6 oz) jars.

Quince Jelly
Tatli s'farjal

3 kg (6 lb 8 oz) quince
5 cups sugar
Juice of 1 lemon

Wash and dry the fruit. Cut each quince in four without peeling them, soaking them immediately in water in a large cooking pan. Remove the seeds from the centre of the fruit and save for later use. Make sure that the quince are covered with water and cook them covered on a high heat until they are soft and you can mash them with the back of a spoon. It takes about one hour. Allow them to cool for one hour then pour out the contents through a fine sieve into another pan. You can crush the pulp in order to obtain more juice. The strained juice will serve as the base for the jelly.

Do not waste the pulp. Save it in a glass bowl and use later to make a dessert.

Strain the juice for a second time by passing it through a fine cloth into a third pan. Measure the sugar and add it to the twice-strained juice then put the pan uncovered on a high heat until it boils. You have to be careful not to let it boil over. Put the seeds you have reserved with two cloves inside a piece of cheesecloth. Tie a knot and throw it in the cooking jelly. Let it cook uncovered for one hour, stirring it every once in a while and at 45 minutes into the cooking check it for consistency. When a small cooled amount in a tilted glass plate rolls without dripping, it is an indication that the jelly is ready. Add the lemon juice and cook for another five minutes then remove it from the heat. Pour out as soon as possible in jars and close them tightly. It makes 5–6 175 g (6 oz) jars.

If you have saved the pulp, add to it a cup of milk, sugar and cinnamon and serve it as a snack for the children instead of having them under your feet waiting until the jelly is ready to spread into sandwiches.

Refreshments

Lemonade with Mint Leaves

Nothing more delectable than this drink on a cool summer afternoon!

She offered me a chair by the kitchen table and disappeared through the service door that led to the garden patch and came back with six lemons and a small bunch of mint leaves. As she squeezed them and stirred the juice with sugar and water in a pitcher, I found myself trying to recollect when last I had had fresh lemonade. She carefully washed a few mint leaves and put them in the pitcher, and from a small bottle that was sitting on a shelf she added two drops of a sweet transparent liquid. She then sat across from me and remained silent. Before she finally took a sip from her drink she pointed to mine as a form of invitation, and I had a spurt of the essential quality of what the earth can offer. It was the two drops of essence of orange blossom that made all the difference.

(Christiane Dabdoub Nasser, *Leyla*)

Ingredients

The juice of 3 lemons (200 cl/7 fl oz)

45 g (2 oz) sugar
700 cl (24.5 fl oz) water
1 tsp essence of orange blossom
A few twigs of tender fresh mint leaves
Thin slices of lemon

Squeeze the lemons and stir in the sugar. Add the water and keep on stirring, making sure that all the sugar has dissolved. Add the mint leaves, essence and a few slices of lemon and refrigerate for an hour or so before serving.

Mulberry Syrup
Sharab tout

3 kg (6 lb 8 oz) very ripe red mulberries
Sugar
2 tbs lemon juice

Wash the mulberries and leave them to drain in a colander for a few minutes. Transfer them to a glass bowl and add one cup of sugar. Mix well and let them sit for three to four hours or until they become soggy. Squeeze them through a cheesecloth bag into a large cooking pan. Depending on the ripeness of the mulberries you might obtain two to three cups juice.

For the syrup add two cups sugar to every cup of mulberry juice while stirring. Cook over a medium heat while stirring until it boils, then cook for 15 minutes. Turn off the heat and let cool before you transfer to sterilised glass bottles. Preserve in a cool dark cabinet.

Tamarind Syrup
Sharab tamarhindi

When I was a little child, during the long hot summer afternoons my mother used to call on friends of hers, originally Jerusalemites who had moved to Bethlehem after the *nakba,* the displacement following the 1948 war. Tradition requires that we address close friends of one's parents as aunt and uncle, the same as with family. Tante Yvonne and Tante Virginie, the two ladies of the house, served the most appetising assortment of home-made biscuits and cakes that I have ever seen. They were reason enough for me to put up with long afternoons with no other children to play with. That and the swing in their backyard.

Daintily arranged on white lace in an old-fashioned silver tray, they were served in summer with different home-made lemonades, which regularly initiated a tedious exchange of recipes and the inevitable comparisons with so and so's baking or art of entertainment. The ritual of *diafeh,* the code of conduct for both host and guests, prescribed a polite acceptance of the things that were offered. There was one thing I most particularly dreaded in this ceremony that announced itself by the tinkling of ice cubes against fine glasses, followed by the appearance of a reddish-brown lemonade. However much I dislike *sharab tamarhindi,* feigning a tummy-ache would have deprived me of the biscuits occupying a large part of the silver tray.

The exotic flavour of tamarind syrup has since then become a favourite of mine!

Ingredients

1 kg (2 lb 4 oz) package of tamarind
4 ltrs (7 pt) water

3 kg (6 lb 8 oz) sugar
2 tbs freshly squeezed lemon juice

Wash the tamarind then soak it in the water for at least seven hours. Work the water with the fruit so as to obtain an almost uniform thick texture and pass it through a juice extractor. It is the best and most efficient way to obtain juice with the least effort. Then pass the liquid through a cheesecloth. Add the sugar and cook over a medium heat stirring constantly until all the sugar is dissolved. Leave it to boil, skimming any foam that forms on the surface with a slotted spoon. Once it starts thickening remove it from the heat and let it cool. Fill in sterilised glass bottles and close with a cork.

This recipe makes about 6 one litre (1 ¾ pt) bottles. Each bottle makes about 15 servings.

Miscellaneous Recipes and Menus

There are as many lifestyles as there are people and any approach to cooking and entertainment necessarily excludes a whole range of diverse possibilities that reflect the intricate mosaic of Palestinian culture. Through a weakness on my part I succumbed to the urge of suggesting menus which, I believe, reflect the different approaches to food among certain Palestinians; however, they should by no means limit your perception of other possibilities which, I hope, have transpired through the introductions to the different sections and the individual dishes.

While most Palestinians prefer to entertain the traditional way, especially for festive and ceremonial occasions, many cooks, mostly among the more cosmopolitan, urban sections of society, also pride themselves on being able to serve international dishes at their table. For a long time they have adopted western practices as a symbol of distinction and sophistication. Lately, however, a renewed consciousness in the value of traditional food has manifested itself at social and family gatherings and serving regional dishes has become quite the thing. This phenomenon is generally rooted in the broad cultural revival that is sweeping Palestine, but it also has to do with an awareness of the worth and appeal of Palestinian cookery and the tremendous opportunities it offers for creativity and refinement.

Light Brunch Menu

Nothing beats a spring or early summer late morning brunch served on the terrace or in the *hadir*, the closed patio, followed by a hubbly-bubbly (the Middle Eastern water-pipe known as *narghileh*) and a game of cards that stretches way into the afternoon.

Brunch parties have become quite common on holidays and weekends. Following is a suggested menu of a light brunch for a small party.

Falafel (chickpea fritters)
Fried eggs with *sumak*
Marinated olives
Labneh, slightly salted and sour cream cheese, served with olive oil and mint leaves.
Zeit u za'tar, a spice mix with a thyme base served with olive oil
Traditional white cheese
Tabun bread, the traditional outdoor clay oven
Mint tea

Fried Eggs with Sumak
Beyd b'sumak

The best way to prepare and serve the eggs is in individual, traditional, shallow clay bowls that go on the stove-top, but if you do not have them use an old-fashioned aluminium frying-pan. For a small pan cook two eggs at a time, to make sure that everyone gets his or her serving piping hot.

Ingredients

2 fresh eggs
4 tbs olive oil
1 tsp *sumak*
Salt and pepper to taste

Heat the olive oil in the pan or in the clay bowl until it sizzles. Add the two eggs and sprinkle with the *sumak*, salt and pepper. Spoon out some of the oil over the eggs until they are cooked to your liking.

Marinated Olives

Many homes pickle their own olives, using the harvest of their own groves or buying them from private landowners who traditionally provide them with their yearly supply. For those who are less fortunate and can only buy their olives off the supermarket shelf, a personal touch can transform such insipid commercial fare to a valuable creation that is likely to impress anyone you serve them to.

Ingredients

1 jar of olives preserved in salted water
2 hot peppers, whole or sliced
6 garlic cloves, peeled and crushed
¼ cup freshly squeezed lemon juice
Enough olive oil to cover the olives

Drain the olives from their liquid. Mix together the garlic, lemon juice and half a cup of oil and add to the olives and mix thoroughly. Add the hot peppers whole or sliced; if you slice them make sure to remove the seeds. Transfer the olives with the dressing to a bigger jar. Add enough olive oil to cover and store for a week away from any source of light or heat.

Once the olives are consumed you can use the left over marinade to dress a salad or to sprinkle over *labneh*.

Labneh

In the old days when milk was not readily available, *labneh* was processed into a thick paste, shaped into balls and preserved in olive oil. That was the way I got used to eating it at my grandmother's. Although I have always preferred the fresh variety, every once in a while I get an urge for preserved *labneh* and indulge my greed by spreading it on toasted whole-wheat bread, the closest version to my grandmother's *tabun* bread.

Whichever way you serve *labneh*, you can be sure that the plate will be wiped clean within a few minutes of serving it. So always be sure to have some back-up for seconds. Spread the *labneh* on a plate forming an edge with the back of a spoon, sprinkle olive oil and add a herb of your choice, fresh or dried: mint leaves, thyme, rosemary or basil. Serve with sliced tomatoes and cucumbers on the side.

Labneh is available in most Middle-Eastern specialty stores, but it is very easy to prepare your own: all you need is a coffee filter and a drip funnel.

Place a large coffee filter in the funnel over a big mug and pour some plain sour yogurt inside the filter. Cover and let it drip, inside the refrigerator, overnight or until you get the *labneh* to desired consistency. Remove from the filter, add some salt to taste and serve with your favourite herb. Do not forget to sprinkle with a generous amount of olive oil.

Copious Brunch Menu

To celebrate a special occasion with a larger crowd of guests, a brunch is quite the 'in' way to entertain, provided you have help or you are organised enough to plan ahead. The items on this menu can easily be prepared ahead. The advantage is that you can serve all the varieties all at once, except for the dessert.

Falafel (chickpea fritters)
Ful m'dammas
Sambousek with meat
Fried white sheep's cheese, served on a bed of greens
Labneh served with olive oil and a variety of fresh herbs on the side
Raw vegetables: cucumbers, tomatoes, spring onions and any other vegetable in season served sliced with *tahineh* dip
Black and green marinated olives
Qras b'za'tar
Tabun bread

For dessert
Tamriyeh or *m'tabbaq*
Tea with aniseed biscuits

Menu for a Mezze Party

Following is a suggested assortment of mezze for an informal gathering. Using the same quantities indicated in the recipes, it can serve 15 people:

Cold salads

Hummos; m'tabbal; foul m'dammas; bakdounsieh; tomatoes with thyme salad; fried aubergines and marrows with yoghurt and pine nuts; traditional *tahineh* salad.

Relishes and pickles

Hot peppers marinated in olive oil; olives marinated in olive oil and garlic; pickled cucumbers, cauliflower and turnips; fresh raw spring onions trimmed and washed.

*Hot pastries (*mou'ajjanat*)*

Sfiha; cheese *sambousek;* meat *sambousek.*

Christmas Eve Dinner Menu

Choice of three salads
Cheese *sambousek*
Sfiha
Moussaka'a
Stuffed chicken
Oriental rice
Choice of steamed vegetables
Esh el'saraya
Ghraybeh
Fruit salad

Large Easter Family Luncheon

Assortment of salads
Artichokes with coriander
Spinach breads
Malfouf
Roasted leg of lamb
Choice of steamed vegetables
Ka'k and *Ma'moul*
Knafeh or *m'hallabiyeh*

Ramadan Iftar Banquet

Dates with *laban*
Chicken soup
Assortment of salads
Pan *kibbeh* with aubergine salad
Sheikh el-mehshi
Fattet djaj
Qatayef
Apricots in syrup
Hetalliyeh

Lenten Large Family Meal

Lentil soup with swiss chard
M'tabbal

Avocado salad
Beet salad
Spinach breads
Okra with tomatoes
Stuffed vine leaves and marrows (*siami*)
Farayek
Apricots in syrup
   Fruit salad

Menu from an Armenian kitchen

The Armenian community has been part of the Palestinian cultural mosaic since the middle of the fifth Century. The first nation to adopt Christianity as its official religion at the beginning of the fourth Century, Armenian pilgrims have flocked to the Holy Land ever since and their presence has been continuous, growing to a significant size right after the Turkish massacre of Armenians in 1915. The third most important Christian community in Palestine, the middle of the nineteenth century witnessed expansion of its territory around the Monastery complex within the old city of Jerusalem and progress in the fields of commerce, education and services to the community and the many pilgrims who flocked there.

Although important demographic changes have occurred within the last fifty years, with many Armenians moving out of the convent complex, and others emigrating to different parts of Europe, America and Australia, the convent will always be the focal point of the Armenian Quarter and the heart of the community.

Bartlett's description of the exterior of the convent area in 1842 is as true today as it was then. The Armenian Quarter has been spared the development projects that have transformed the other quarters of Jerusalem into shabby tourist sites and kitschy residential areas:

> The only building in Jerusalem that presents any considerable appearance of comfort; the compactly built façade, the neatly paved street in front, overshadowed by noble trees, and the portly and highly respectable looking monks about its doorway, are all redolent of ease, and wealth, and cleanliness rare in the city of Jerusalem.
>
> (Bartlett, *Walks*)

One and a half centuries later, William Dalrymple's impressions testify to the preserved authenticity of that section of the Old City:

> The Armenian Quarter is very different. It is easy to pass it by without realising its existence. It is a city within a city, entered through its own gate and bounded by its own high, butter coloured wall.
>
> The gatehouse gives onto a warren of tunnels and passageways. Off one of these I have been given an old groin-vaulted room smelling of dust and old age, with a faint whiff of medieval church. In the streets around my room, hidden behind anxiously twitching lace curtains, lives a displaced population, distinct from their neighbours in language, religion, history and culture.
>
> (William Dalrymple, *From the Holy Mountain*)

Armenian food as it is cooked in Jerusalem does not call for a particular variety of spices, one explanation being that the Armenian community adopted a lot of the local culinary culture. Fenugreek, however, is particularly Armenian and is the basic spice used in the preparation of *basturma*, a spicy dried meat available in most Armenian restaurants of Jerusalem and Bethlehem. However, only a select few are lucky to benefit from the *basturma* prepared in the kitchens of the convent.

When Armenians meet for a festive meal, the food is guaranteed to be abundant, the noise ear shattering and the singing maudlin. An Armenian Christmas menu follows.

Assortment of salads
Basturma
Stuffed artichokes
White beans casserole
Meat and cheese *sumbousek*
Pot roast
Choice of vegetables
Armenian *helve*
Anush abur (wheat pudding)

Index